T0285294

Praise for *The Woman They Wanted*

"Shannon's story will captivate you. Her brave, brilliant, and beautiful narrative smashes the myth of biblical womanhood, and her courage will help women trapped in purity culture find hope for a better life."

—Beth Allison Barr, James Vardaman Professor of History at Baylor University and author of *The Making of Biblical Womanhood*

"In silken prose and boundary-shattering perceptions, Shannon Harris tells her story of ascending, alongside her famous husband, to the heights of the Evangelical world only to learn—slowly, painfully, honestly, triumphantly—that who she was had gotten lost. *The Woman They Wanted* will become the vanguard of a new movement of women rediscovering themselves, their dreams, and their futures. This book will grieve you, anger you, and inspire you. In one word: stunning. I could not put this book down."

—Scot McKnight, author of *A Church Called Tov* and *The Jesus Creed*

"For anyone who has felt limited by the pressures to conform and self-sacrifice for someone else's ideals, may you find solidarity in the pages of this book. Shannon's story is one of liberation and courage, of casting aside the expectations built by a church culture intertwined with patriarchy, power, and control. Most importantly, this book is about finding your voice again. May Shannon's story of courage call forth the brave within you as well."

—Tara Teng, author of *Your Body Is a Revolution*

"The title says it all: *The Woman They Wanted.* This book is a must-read for anyone wanting to understand and get a glimpse into the life of women in the church, and especially those who are married to the leadership. I couldn't put it down because Shannon's story is so honestly and poetically written as she shares how she had to be what they wanted rather than who she actually is."

—David Hayward, artist behind the
@NakedPastor and author of *Flip It Like This!*

"*The Woman They Wanted* reveals the dark underbelly of how evangelicalism views women and its degrading efforts to silence, shame, and mold women into submissive, oppressed shells of themselves—all billed as 'God's plan.' In her own story of healing from high-control religion, Harris shares her journey of picking up the pieces that were discarded in favor of becoming a 'good woman' and finding peace and wholeness within herself."

—Laura Anderson, founder of the Center
for Trauma Resolution and Recovery

"So many women know what it's like to play the part of the 'good woman' while slowly losing their sparkle and soul. Shannon has so much sparkle and soul, and her story of spending decades being 'the woman they wanted' and of how she found her way back to her authentic self will be a catalyst for many other women to say YES to their own journey of freedom. If you grew up in the church and never felt permission to be the woman you wanted to be, read this book!"

—Morgan Day Cecil, creator of the Feminine Wholeness® Method

THE WOMAN THEY WANTED

THE WOMAN THEY WANTED

SHATTERING THE ILLUSION OF THE GOOD CHRISTIAN WIFE

Shannon Harris

Broadleaf Books
Minneapolis

THE WOMAN THEY WANTED
Shattering the Illusion of the Good Christian Wife

Some names and identifying details have been changed to protect the privacy of individuals featured in the book.

Library of Congress Control Number 2022056977 (print)

Cover design: Michele Lenger / 1517 Media

Print ISBN: 978-1-5064-8316-0
eBook ISBN: 978-1-5064-8317-7

Printed in China

The most destructive cultural conditions for a woman to be born into and to live under are those that insist on obedience without consultation with one's soul. Those with no loving forgiveness rituals, those that force a woman to choose between soul and society, those where compassion for others is walled off by economic tiers or caste systems, where the body is seen as something needing to be "cleaned' or as a shrine to be regulated by fiat, where the new, the unusual, or the different engenders no delight, and where curiosity and creativity are punished and denigrated instead of rewarded, or only rewarded if one is not a woman, where painful acts are perpetrated on the body and called holy, or whenever a woman is punished unjustly, as Alice Miller puts it succinctly, "for her own good," where the soul is not recognized as being its own right.

Clarissa Pinkola Estes, PhD

To my parents, Mitzi Ash and Milt Hendrickson.

CONTENTS

PREFACE

I HAVE LEARNED the hard way that fear is a miserable cage. And though it is an invisible one, its bars can feel as strong as iron. I know this because I spent a decade or more of my life afraid. Whether you are afraid of something inside of you or outside of you the way out is the same, and that is directly through it. That is easier said than done, but it is how you will find your courage. No one can give you courage. Not really. You enter courage, and then you collect it. You'll see what I mean someday. But it is worth it, getting braver.

I wasn't always afraid. I was a bold and spunky child. I loved to stand on the beach where the waves broke—the more threatening the wave the better. I loved the thrill of it. No matter how massive they loomed over my pint-sized frame I knew I could make myself a nimble arrow, dive through the center, and reemerge victorious on the other side. I was convinced I was stronger than the waves, and in a way I was. Because I knew how the waves thought and how they behaved, and I knew my way through them.

But then again I *had* been prepared for it. My father was a swimmer, and the water had always been a part of my life. My earliest memories of conquering fear were being coaxed off a diving board with my dad treading below promising to catch me, or being perched atop his back while he swam us so far out in the ocean I was certain we'd be lunch for a shark. But my father, with his cool, natural confidence, would chuckle as if to say, "Nothing to fear here. I've got you." He always made me feel safe.

I think it is easier to navigate a world that we know. A familiar environment, with familiar people. But the unknown world alone? How does a person, particularly a woman, prepare for that? A church world for which she has no context or history? Dorothy was not at ease in Oz until she got to the end of the Yellow Brick Road. Princess Diana took years to find her way out of the British monarchy. Alice was out of sorts in Wonderland until she found the key. It takes time to find the way.

Every day countless people enter into a new life-changing situation—a job, a relationship, motherhood, an unexpected move to a new country. We sometimes go in thinking it will be one thing only to discover it is really quite another. There is little time to prepare for the force of this kind of change. Little chance to work out your choices or prevent the upending of life as you once knew it. From the moment of our arrival in this new situation, it feels as though we might sink or swim.

This was me in a world I knew as *church*. As a twenty-three-year-old singer-performer and soon-to-be wife of an internationally known author and megachurch pastor, nothing in my past experience could possibly have prepared me for what was to come. It was a wave that caught me completely off guard, sending me topsy-turvy and tumbling. It was not until years later, when I finally managed to find the shore, that I grasped the whole of what had happened. Like the groggy coming-to from a drug-induced dream.

It was a mistake so innocent and common it is almost laughable now. A young woman so captivated by her desire for someone or something that she trades her soul to get it, only to realize later at what cost to herself. I became the woman the church leaders wanted, betraying myself in the process, until I was a fragment of the woman I knew myself to be.

Imagine my surprise when I happened upon stories of women with experiences similar to mine. Women like me who had struggled to disentangle themselves from patriarchy, or had experienced a profound awakening, or a metamorphosis from one self to another. I discovered these stories in books that became companions on my journey to reclaim my true self. The wisdom of these authors along with a few trusted confidants validated my experiences and at times gave me names to put to feelings and ideas for which I had no vocabulary.

I have come to learn that my church experience is sadly representative of many others' experience. The criticism I present of my own church does not mean I condemn all churches, Christianity in general, or other religions.

Suffice it to say, Christianity spans a wide range of beliefs and practices and cultural and political differences. It's not surprising that under the mantle of Christianity there are multitudes of true believers in conflict with other true believers.

The history of Christianity is one of divisions and schisms, competing doctrines and controversy, and those claiming to be true Christians. Christianity is and likely always will be in the eye of the beholder. As a layperson, but seasoned pastor's wife of fifteen years who has played many roles, I have sought to avoid confusing my experience at my church with hasty generalizations about Christianity. Forgive me when I fail to heed humorist Mark Twain's observation: "All generalizations are false, including this one."

This book is the result of my journey—the story of a young woman who makes a series of choices that gradually change her into someone she doesn't know. It is not a book about religion so much as it is a woman's story, my story within a church and within patriarchy. Most importantly, it is a book about protecting the vital connection we each need to have to ourselves, our values, and our dreams. It is my hope that the book will inspire women and other readers to live more courageously and authentically wherever they are.

Part One

BEGINNINGS

starving.

IT WAS A Sunday morning after breakfast, and my husband was preaching in a few hours. My three children were somewhere in our four-thousand-square-foot colonial in the suburbs. My husband was the pastor of a large, conservative American evangelical church, and I was *His Wife*.

At this point, we had been on staff at the church for nearly fifteen years. And when I say "we," what I really mean is he. I was not on staff. My husband was on staff. Only men were pastors there. But for some reason every move I made mattered—as if his job depended on it. That is the way it always was. But I did not get paid for all this mattering. I had not minded that before, but I was starting to. It was not so much about the money, though the money would have been nice. It was more about the mattering.

My husband, Joshua, was the hip young guy hired to carry the church through the next generation. He was the head pastor now, and our church was the mothership church in a growing network of churches. We were Reformed Charismatic. It was a whole brand.

On this particular Sunday, I was having a breakdown. Or more like, I was sending out an SOS.

You should know that up until this point in my life—my church life, that is—I had been mostly unconscious. Not literally, but figuratively. I didn't know you could be unconscious and at the same time think you are living your life, but you can. But my depression was changing that. It was forcing me to pay attention to myself, and it was only getting worse. I was crying all the time and hiding it from my friends. I had to figure out what the cause was before I ruined everything. My three kids needed me.

I wondered if I was going crazy because I kept seeing the same exact scene in my mind. Months would go by and I'd forget about it, but the scene always returned. It was me, but instead of me I was a gnarly, hungry old beggar woman in a burlap dress with long, frizzy hair. The beggar woman was crawling on the floor searching for crumbs. Whenever she found one, she pulled it close to her chest and looked over her shoulder anxiously, worried that someone might steal it from her.

A few years from that day, I would know exactly why I was having this vision.

I lost myself trying to be good for other people. I was trying to be the woman they wanted. I was happy to do it at one time, but not anymore. I had nothing left to give. The crumbs were the last little bits of me I was trying to hold onto. I was starving for my life.

That Sunday I called to my husband, who was downstairs preparing his sermon in his office, which was next to the *Great Room*. The *Great Room* was where we hosted our twenty-some pastors and their wives about once a month. I asked my husband to come up to my bedroom because I had something important to tell him. I met him at the door. I was trying to make a scene, but a quiet one because I didn't want to alarm the kids. They were twelve, ten, and six.

I said I wasn't going to church that day, that I needed him to take the kids, and that I was locking myself in our bedroom and wasn't coming out for three whole days. And I said I wasn't sure I could keep going to church anymore. At that, his eyes widened for a second. I could see the wheels turning in his head, but not much ever rattled my husband. He was the oldest of seven children, and I often said he was the best mother in the house. He looked at me and said okay and then turned to head downstairs to handle the fray. It wasn't exactly the response I was hoping for. I shut the bedroom door and took my computer from the dresser where I'd left it. I walked over to my bed, slid my hand underneath the mattress, and took out the book on Catholicism I had hidden there. Then I settled onto the bed to look for answers.

• • •

My mother knew the place was trouble from the very start. On her very first visit to church I was giving my testimony. That's where I stood up to tell everyone my story of how I'd come to believe in God and why I was now a changed person forever. The pastors of the church had asked me to share my story on a Sunday morning for the service and I had invited both of my parents to attend. It was maybe a year after I started coming to church. During my testimony, I talked about how my parents' divorce had been difficult for me and how I'd been able to make peace with it.

After I spoke and the sermon was over, CJ, the head pastor, invited those in the congregation whose lives had been affected by divorce to come forward to "receive ministry." Often, this just meant prayer. But sometimes, like that day, it meant Bob. Bob was the music pastor and an extraordinary pianist and musician. Earlier in his career he had created and developed a highly successful Christian music group. Bob was CJ's other half and, in my opinion, a huge reason for the success of the ministry. Many churches have a charismatic leader, but they also need to have heart. They need vulnerability. Bob could make a room of ten thousand people feel intimate and personal. CJ may have been the one to first attract people, but it was Bob who kept them there.

Bob had a special gift for making up songs spontaneously, in real time, with no advance preparation. The church called them *prophetic songs*. They were complete with story, meaning, melody, and rhyme. Bob would sing them in the first person, as if it were God speaking. There was something magical, emotional, and powerful about these songs. If the intent was to get an emotional response from people, it worked, and CJ seemed to take full advantage of this. If he wanted a prophetic song after a sermon, all he had to do was cue Bob with a look from across the stage to order it.

On the day I was giving my testimony, CJ did want one. And as I mentioned, those who had been affected by divorce had gathered at the front of the stage. Bob started to play the piano while collecting his thoughts, and then he began to sing. It didn't take long before half of us were crying. Someone handed me a tissue. When the song was finished we all went back to our seats. *Wrecked for God.*

When the service ended we walked out to the lobby and to my surprise my mother turned and placed herself squarely in front of me. She was abrupt and sharp with a warning, which was out of the ordinary for her; she isn't one to interfere. But she wanted me to hear that she didn't trust the church. She thought it was disingenuous and manipulative. I brushed her off and came to Bob and CJ's defense, and then we went out for lunch. And for the next two decades my mother never said another word.

My mother has never been wrong. Not yet anyway.

• • •

Downstairs, I heard a new voice in the kitchen. It was Bev, a woman from church who babysat for us on occasion. *Josh must have called her to help with the kids. God bless her.* A few minutes later I heard the side door shut, and the house went quiet. I was alone now.

I googled the "Five Points of Calvinism," half-thinking maybe I should just change religions. Church had started out so positive (or so I thought) but over the years our church doctrine had veered more and more Calvinist and in my opinion, it hadn't been good for anyone. The Puritans were Calvinists, and they sure didn't seem happy. Maybe that was the problem.

Calvinism's essential teaching is called *total depravity*, which teaches that people are corrupt to the core. Even the good that comes from a person is said to be God acting from within them and not the actual person. It was a very depressing way to live. It meant that even if you did something nice for someone, like buying them a latte, you had to be sure to remind yourself that it wasn't your idea. *Good job, Shannon! Just don't forget the latte was God's idea and not yours, because nothing good comes from you, k?* It's because of Calvinism that I now pay my therapist hundreds of dollars to remind me that I'm fabulous.

To be fair, not everything was terrible at church. There was a lot of good too. Like the people. So many good people. The all-in types.

I was half-seriously considering becoming a Catholic. My grandmother was Catholic, so there was family history there. They also had tangibles like beads and candles. Things you could actually touch, which sounded nice for some reason. Frankly, our pastors didn't consider Catholics real Christians. They said the Catholics placed too much importance on Mary. I wasn't sure I cared what our pastors thought anymore.

The theologians in our camp had the right answers to everything. Everything. Actually, they had been right about too many things for too many years. It started to give them away because everybody knows no one can be that right all of the time. If they had at least thrown in a few *I don't knows* in the mix, maybe I would have gone on for another decade. But no one else was doing Christianity right enough or hard enough or biblical enough, and their unquestionable certainty had grown tiresome. I wasn't just skeptical. I was tired.

I was really, really, really tired.

church.

THERE ARE CHURCHES and then there are circuses.

CJ, whose official name is Charles Joseph Mahaney, was a young twentysomething when he founded the church along with Larry Tomzack, a man about ten years his senior. CJ was a self-professed former pothead who hadn't bothered to finish college. The two met sometime during the hippie Jesus movement. By 1982 they weren't just building a church, they were building a denomination and a name for themselves. A movement, a brand.

It started as a small, tight-knit group of young adults in the Washington, DC, area meeting in somebody's home. Just a bunch of young people casually getting together for fellowship and prayer. But then those young adults married each other and became young families. And young families attracted more young families. And soon they were a growing church. They moved the Sunday services out of the living room and into school auditoriums. Eventually, they saved enough money to buy some land in the suburbs and build. They called it *Covenant Life Church.*

In simplest terms, the church was evangelical (think Billy Graham) and charismatic (think faith healings and people falling over) and Reformed (think Puritans who, you may recall, hung a bunch of women, most likely for getting sick from a fungus in the rye). The charismatic part was the emotion. The Reformed part was the tradition. And then there was female submission.

As the church grew, so did the vision of its leaders. They added a publishing branch and a music branch. CJ started the Pastor's College and began training and sending out men to plant churches. Bob trained men to be music leaders. All the while Covenant Life

Church remained the blueprint and model for all the other churches in the ministry to follow. They called it People of Destiny International, which definitely sounded strange to me at first, but the people were so very nice and normal I got used to it. When I heard they were planning on changing the name I assumed it was because they wanted something sensible, but it may have been to escape the past or get a fresh start. Eventually, the name was changed to Sovereign Grace Ministries. At that time, there were roughly eighty churches across the country under the Sovereign Grace umbrella.

I don't think the church intended to become as unhealthy as it did. It appears to have gradually and quietly headed in that direction. As the church grew, so did CJ's power within it. He began lording over his flock. He used his position and power to serve his own needs and not the needs of his congregation. He surrounded himself with younger men who idolized him, and he trained them as leaders. He asked that they protect him from scrutiny. And he was quick to cut off relationships with those who did not show him the loyalty and admiration he felt he deserved. And most significant was what I would come to learn later. CJ's misconduct would become public through some six hundred pages of evidence compiled by a former associate, titled *The Documents*. In the months that followed, CJ's leadership was again (as it still is) noticeably absent in matters pertaining to allegations of sexual abuse cover-up that would have occurred during his time of leadership.

This was a leader who rose to his position because he was charismatic and could hold the attention of a crowd. I'm not aware that he had any qualifications beyond that. He did not attend seminary or divinity school. But somehow he ended up in the role of a shepherd when he might have been better suited for a career as a used-car salesman or an actor. Did he even believe in God? Who really knows? If you think about it, being a pastor-celebrity is a pretty sweet job. People give you 10 percent of their income and you hardly have to ask.

You get lot of attention, but the job is far more stable than an acting career. Besides, you can put on an act anytime you want. You can pretend to care and love others.

Whatever the case, in reflecting on the entirety of my experience at Covenant Life Church, no other single individual's ideas and behavior bring more clarity or understanding to the broader context of the stories I share in this book.

cj.

MY MOTHER SAYS that the first time I introduced her to CJ, which we think was at my wedding, he didn't look into her eyes. She never forgot that.

For me, now, CJ lives in my mind as a caricature of himself. He's on a stage wearing black coattails and a top hat, looking out with a sly smile as he performs his tricks. He is the Ringmaster. The Salesman. The Magician. He quickly builds a house out of cards and whoosh! It's back in his hand again as a full deck. Look, now he's making something new! We are all mesmerized, and our eyes are fixed on his waving and shouting and antics. The show moves on at a steady clip, so there is no time to process. His stories keep us laughing or crying, but most of all they keep our eyes glued on him. We are too busy being entertained and hoping for a chance to participate in the fun to realize that we are growing old.

• • •

I believed him back then, on the stage. And I believed he believed the words he preached. Off the stage, though, I was seeing things more accurately. He was different on the ground. Distant. He looked through me whenever we spoke, and I could tell that he didn't truly see me. His smile went no deeper than the curve of his lips.

After one particular Sunday service people came forward for prayer. Leaders were already positioned along the perimeter of the stage ready to greet them and pray. CJ was standing on the stage of course, which was nearly five feet high, and he was towering over everyone below. I was standing just a few feet behind him because I had sung that morning. I got caught up watching him as he matched up people *wanting* prayer with people *available* for prayer. He was reaching down toward people's heads and swooshing people together using large arm gestures to accomplish this. He was very focused on this work, and I wondered why he felt the need to do that. Surely grown adults could manage to get a prayer without assistance from him above? I couldn't help but wonder if he was avoiding praying for people. Of all the people who should be on the ground praying, shouldn't it be the pastor of the church?

When I began singing for the church, CJ started introducing me before my solos. He would make a big deal of it and call me the *girl who gave up her dreams for the local church.* I don't remember ever stating that as a fact. I even visited Nashville during this time to sing for someone in the music industry, thanks to a connection I made at church. But most people discouraged me from moving and pursuing acting and singing. Music careers were "worldly," and Hollywood was overflowing with sin and debauchery. And anyway, women were supposed to get married and have children. There had been a lot of pressure to give up my dreams. That pressure just floated in the air. Air pressure.

Because CJ was introducing me this way, people in the church were constantly praising me. They would say how wonderful it was of me to give up my dreams for the local church, which felt good. Later I would realize that by calling me that, CJ actually called that reality into being. He was naming me.

CJ named other things besides people. He had phrases that he used often for dramatic effect. He called the church *the dearest place on earth.* He called the church bookstore the *world's greatest bookstore.* When someone asked CJ how he was, his standard reply was, "Better than I deserve."

It's a powerful thing, naming someone. Giving a newborn baby a name that they will use for the rest of their life? The name will shape the child's life forever. But creating a name to shape someone's identity? It's even more powerful. It is not just shaping what a person will be called, but who that person will be. It is like those movies where the father has planned for the son to take over the family bakery. But the son does not want to be a baker, he wants to be a boxer. So he spends the whole movie tearing himself away from his father's story for his life—from the name his father had given him. This kind of naming oversteps the boundary line where one person ends and another begins. It is handing them a story and asking them to tell it as their own. CJ had a story for my life, and I started to believe that story was true.

childhood.

MY FAMILY LIVED in a small seaside town in New Jersey. Our neighborhood nudged right up to the edge of the water. We were the quintessential white, upper-middle-class American family. A father, a mother, two children—one boy and one girl—and a Siamese cat. My father worked for IBM. He'd come home from work in a gray pinstripe suit with a briefcase in his hand, change into shorts and a t-shirt, and head out for his evening run before dinner.

My father adored the water, and growing up we usually owned a boat. In the summers we rented a house for two weeks on Long Beach Island. I was too young to waterski then, but I can recall being bundled in my mother's lap, her arms wrapped around me tight, with the boat beating and scudding its way across the chop. Wind whipping my hair across my face.

My mother played tennis, and I can picture her wearing a white tennis skirt and white Tretorn sneakers with a yellow logo. She wore those white ankle socks with the pom-poms on the back and a white sun visor too. We'd ride up to the tennis courts, and while she played a match I would spend the time running between the courts and a nearby beach. I reveled in the fact that I could run around freely, totally unsupervised. (I wasn't.) My brother, Scott, three years older than me, was usually riding his bike around the neighborhood with his friends or getting ready for baseball.

When I was three, the Montessori teacher told my mother she was sure I would grow up to be a singer or an actress. She said that in her classroom of thirty children my voice carried over everyone else's. (Then she probably took two Tylenol.) My mother thinks one of the reasons I am musical is because she was taking piano lessons while she was pregnant with me. Her teacher believed in teaching piano using real music only, so my mother learned the basics with Satie's *Gymnopédie* and Beethoven's *Moonlight Sonata*. Of course she had me take piano lessons too.

When I was five, my parents took me into New York City to see the original production of *Annie* on Broadway and I was never the same after that. I wanted to be Annie. I needed to be on that stage.

I came home from New York and taught myself to sing with my record player and three vinyl albums. Two of the albums were the musicals *Annie* and *Oklahoma*. The third album was, ironically, a collection of feminist songs and stories my mother had given me—*Free to Be You and Me*. It featured a number of artists—Marlo Thomas, Alan Alda, Roberta Flack, and Michael Jackson, to name a few. The album sought to point a post-1960s America toward gender neutrality. The songs promoted values like individuality, tolerance, and comfort with one's own identity. The album most definitely shaped early thoughts I had about myself as a human being and as a woman and gave me a framework for how I viewed the world. It also happened to be great for learning character acting.

Cami was my best friend in New Jersey. There was much to love about Cami, but I especially loved that whenever we sang the duet between Daddy Warbucks and Annie she always let me be Annie. We had it all choreographed, and I directed our rehearsals as if we had a performance coming up next week at the Met. Singing and dancing that song with her is one of my happiest childhood memories. Another friend of mine would come over, and we'd dress up in leotards and tutus and stand on the coffee table belting Kenny Rogers's "The Gambler."

I taught myself to sing out in the garage. The sound out there was amplified and I felt electric as I listened to my own sound bouncing off the cement walls and floor all around me. I pressed and pushed my voice to discover what it could and couldn't do. I copied everything I heard from the smallest inflection to a flare on a note to a particular tone or timbre. I felt my own power when I sang.

At Girl Scout camp I understood harmony for the first time. On the last night of camp we were all circled around the flagpole after the flag ceremony. A couple of counselors broke out singing John Denver's "Perhaps Love," and the tight harmonies they used caught my attention. I was mesmerized by the way their voices layered and intertwined over and under each other. The next day on the three-hour car ride home I required my mother to sing the melody on repeat while I worked out the harmony part.

In the sixth grade the music director at the neighboring high school needed six munchkins for his production of *The Wiz.* When my teacher asked if anyone was interested in auditioning, my arm shot up. The day of the audition couldn't come soon enough for me. It was my first time on a real stage. While I was waiting for my turn I looked down at the floor to distract myself and noticed the deep nicks and paint splatters everywhere. I wanted to know more about the stories held in those markings. When my name was called I walked confidently to the designated place in the middle of the stage. I knew I could nail Annie any day of the week. The director, Mr. Crawford, was sitting high on a chair in the otherwise empty orchestra pit about fifteen feet away. A few people sat in the audience. I sang "Tomorrow" and became a munchkin.

When I got to high school, Mr. Crawford told me he'd been waiting for me. He had developed the only performing arts program in the city, and half of my schedule was filled with music. He invested a great deal in me over the next four years and was upset when I didn't choose to go to music school. I'm not sure he ever forgave me. But I didn't want to sing opera, I wanted to go to Broadway. Mr. Crawford said I was too short for Broadway, and I was too scared to move to New York City alone at that time. Plus, in my family it was an advancement of things past for a female to get a college degree. It was never a discussion that I might not go. So off to college I went.

family.

MY FATHER HAS always had a strong, quiet presence about him. At five foot ten and muscular my dad was handsome by anybody's standards. His childhood was a difficult one: his biological father, an elite fighter pilot, died during World War II when my father was just six weeks old. If you compare photographs of my dad and his father, they almost look like they could be the same person. The stress of it all caused my grandmother's milk to dry up, so she kept my dad alive with bananas.

Mums is what I called her, though her name was Elise. I was always mesmerized by her. I call her the photographer-explorer grandmother because she took trips to exotic places like Africa, India, and the Galápagos Islands all by herself. By the time I knew her she had remarried, and I thought it was bold of her to leave her husband behind.

Mums was beautiful enough for Hollywood. Slender and five feet tall with soft, wavy hair and a slight Georgia accent. I can picture her standing just outside her kitchen door, taking a break from cooking, smoking a cigarette, and looking effortlessly chic in a drapey silk outfit or a pair of khakis and a white button shirt. Her home was as interesting as she was: photographs of birds and other images from her travels, seashell collections labeled on glass displays, pinecone and nut wreaths she'd made, and stacks of yellow *National Geographic* magazines. I think Mums had a bit of a wild side to her, and I like to think she gave it to me.

• • •

My own mother was playful, smart, athletic, and nurturing. But out of nowhere she could also shock you with her pragmatic, no-nonsense attitude. As a young girl, she attended a strict, all-girls Catholic school in Annapolis near her mother's job at the State House. My mother's father was a retired Naval officer with a drinking problem, so it was her mother who provided stability and finances for the family.

The highlight of my mother's side of the family was undoubtedly the crab feast held in the backyard of my grandmother's house on Kent Island. Every August the entire family gathered there for a reunion. Long rows of picnic tables would be covered in old *Baltimore Sun* newspapers. Bushel baskets of crabs slathered in Old Bay seasoning were piled high in the center of each table. The whole yard buzzed with people young, old, and everything in between. We'd spend hours hammering away, drinking beer (or soda for the kids), and enjoying ourselves. We looked like a Norman Rockwell scene.

For the most part, my parents chose to raise us without religion. Although my brother and I were baptized in the Episcopal Church as infants, that was as far as it went really. My mother was determined not to raise us with the strict Catholic upbringing she had growing up, and my dad was more than happy to go along with that. He didn't want to repeat much of anything from his childhood.

As a little girl, I noticed that when it came to religion things were a little different at my grandmother's house. You couldn't miss the crosses and rosaries hanging above each bed, the framed pictures of Jesus, and Mary figurines. These obviously meant something more to my grandmother, but whenever I asked my mother about it her distaste for Catholicism kept her answers short. So I occasionally tagged along to church with friends to fill in the gaps. I found my way to Christmas Eve services, youth group trips, bar mitzvahs, and at least one very wild, charismatic service. I think it wasn't religion I was interested in as much as knowledge about people and cultures.

I even "got saved" once by accident. I had been invited to a small youth group meeting by a friend. There were about six of us sitting on the floor of the church, and I was the only newcomer. We sat in a small circle listening while the youth pastor delivered a mini-sermon.

Afterward he had us all close our eyes and bow our heads. He asked us to raise our hands if we thought we'd ever done anything bad. At least that's how I heard the question. I couldn't think of anything especially awful I had ever done, but I thought, *Sure, I've done something bad. Haven't we all?* I was thinking along the lines of a piece of candy I stole when I was three. Or the time I put my brother's hand in hot water while he was sleeping to see if he would wet the bed. So I raised my hand.

But when I opened my eyes all the other kids began congratulating me. I knew they thought I'd made a profession of faith, which I hadn't, and I was angry that they'd all been watching me when their eyes were supposed to be closed. I didn't want anything to do with religion after that.

moving.

AT THE END of first grade the foyer was suddenly filled with moving boxes. We were leaving our idyllic life in New Jersey and moving back to my dad's hometown in Maryland, where my dad was going to work in the family insurance business. My mother pleaded with him for us to stay through the summer. My dad insisted that we move. We moved. It was 1980.

My mom was different in Maryland. I'd wake up and find her sitting at the kitchen table in her burgundy zip-up robe with a strong cup of black coffee, brooding. She wasn't her fun-loving, tennis-playing self here.

Two years later my parents invited my older brother and me into the family room to tell us they were getting a divorce. My dad tried to make it sound exciting by saying I could take the bus over to visit him. I ran upstairs to cry. Now I understand why we frequented this quiet dive of a Chinese restaurant in the months leading up to the announcement. While my brother and I were skewering pork pieces over our tiny table fire pit, my parents were planning their marital exit.

The announcement utterly shocked me. There had been no warning signs so that we would have seen it coming, except perhaps the mood around dinner time. Quiet with a heavy touch of somber. I remember the smell of white wine and a sad, Jane Olivor record playing on repeat in the background. I knew I wanted to make music like that someday.

It was the only major crack in my otherwise extremely fortunate childhood. To my parents' credit they understood *Conscious Uncoupling* long before Gwyneth Paltrow had ever heard of it. They separated amicably, and if there was any drama I never knew.

My mother went back to school and got a master's degree in counseling. Dinners got simpler. No more of my favorite, chicken croquettes, after that. Those involved roasting a chicken, pulling the meat off the bone, making a mixture, shaping, breading, and frying them. Now my mother was up in her room reading and writing papers. When she got her degree and was offered a good job at a college in another city (paying six dollars an hour) she needed to take it. As things got sorted out, it made more sense for my brother and me to stay in our hometown rather than uproot again, so we landed on an unconventional arrangement—two kids living with their dad. Just before the start of junior high I moved in with my dad and brother, where I stayed through college.

girlfriends.

I WAS VERY attached to my mother as a child, and inwardly I was grieving not having her close on a daily basis. Being the only girl at home with an introverted father and a busy older brother meant I processed much of my teenage angst alone, so again I looked to my friends and their families to fill in some of the gaps. Lauren, Julie, Kathy—those were my girls. I met Lauren in the second grade, and she was the closest thing I had to a sister. When we moved up to middle school, Lauren and I met Julie and Kathy. For the rest of our school years the four of us wove closely in and around each other's lives. First periods, first boyfriends, first times. We saw each other through it all. If I strung those girls together like pearls on a necklace and hung it around my neck, I'd almost be wearing my whole life.

Maybe it was because I was surrounded at home by men, but I could never shake the feeling that girls at school knew feminine secrets that I didn't have. They swooshed their hair and walked with their hips swaying and wore outfits that seemed more coordinated than mine. They had cute shoes and girly bedrooms with fluffy pillows and accessories hanging all over the place. Their mothers made dinner every night and mothered (and smothered) them while we kept a steady rotation of restaurants, takeout, and Lean Cuisines, and I had no curfew. I saw and felt the difference between a home with a woman in it and a home without one, and I wanted to be certain which was the right one. The church was more than happy to provide an answer.

alice in wonderland.

THE SUMMER AFTER I graduated college I was in that misty land between dependence and adulthood. I had graduated with a degree in communication, but I was trying to figure out how to go about a career in the performing arts. I decided I'd better learn some guitar because I was planning on moving to Nashville. Through the friend of a friend, I hired a guy my age who had just graduated with a degree in classical guitar. We got a gig at a restaurant together and became friends, and at the same time he began to evangelize me.

At first, I was firm. I told him I wasn't interested in church, I didn't believe in God and I never would. Plus, I would be in Nashville by the end of the summer. But my friend persisted in engaging me on the subject, and after a while I thought maybe I was being closed-minded, so eventually I agreed to visit the church with him. I told myself I would just peek in briefly to see what it was all about, which, you may remember, just happens to be the same exact thing Alice said before she fell down a long and winding rabbit hole.

Part Two

ILLUSIONS

synchrony.

IN LATE AUGUST, the hottest month of the year, my friend arrived to pick me up for my first church visit. As I approached the car, he looked like he was about to say something but held it back. I noticed he glanced at my outfit. I was wearing a light blue baby-doll dress and sandals. Baby-doll dresses are short. The hem of my dress landed a good six or seven inches above my knees. It *was* August in Maryland.

The church was a little over a half-hour away. We drove up to a pleasant but utilitarian brown brick building. We parked, went inside, and made our way through the lobby to the one-thousand-seat auditorium, which was almost filled except for a few back rows. The service had already started as we shimmied our way into some available seats. I looked around. Clearly, I was underclothed.

The music was loud and, to my surprise, quite good. The whole congregation sang and moved almost as if it had been rehearsed. Arms went up during the choruses. Arms went down for the verses. Then back up and back down again. *Impressive synchrony,* I thought.

During the quieter moments people did different things. Some people held their arms out in front with their palms facing up. Some people had their hands folded in prayer. Some were kneeling on the floor. I didn't believe in God, so I was watching everyone closely to see where they thought God was.

The stage was massive and about five feet high. Twelve or so pastors stood on the stage, worshipping. I looked at their profiles. I found them distracting and wondered why they weren't sitting with the common people. I thought pastors were the go-between between God and humans. They appeared to be put there to demonstrate to the rest of us how to sing and pray and bow to God correctly.

Aside from the questionable arm-raising thing, everyone at this church looked normal, although no one else was in a baby-doll dress. In fact, everyone in this church looked a lot like me. Middle-class, intelligent, college-educated, mostly white. *People like this actually believe Bible stories are true? Adam and Eve? The world created in six days?* They were nice stories but impossible to be real. There was no way all those animals could get on an ark and not eat each other alive. And the story of Adam and Eve didn't sound too far off from the *Grimm's Fairy Tales* I had read as a child. Still, it was persuasive—seeing so many people so obviously convinced.

After the sermon the tone of the service changed. The music team came back up, and the pastor invited us to come to the front for prayer if we thought God wanted us to. It was a mystery to me how anyone on earth could possibly know what God wanted.

Just after the service ended, a cheery girl about my age with a huge, warm smile on her face came bouncing toward me. She was so purposeful and friendly I jogged my memory wondering if I should have recognized her from somewhere. I didn't. Two more girls joined us, and they all formed a semicircle around me. They were super friendly, smiling, and warm. Love bombs.

In the car heading home my friend asked me what I thought of the church. I thought, *I've never seen anything like it.* And, *I'm totally exhausted.* Like I'd just attended a wedding and a funeral all in the same day. We drove the rest of the way in quiet, but I could feel the weight of my friend's wanting. Wanting me to like it.

shelley.

MAYBE IF I hadn't met Shelley I would have left sooner. We met at a picnic the singles pastor and his wife were hosting in their backyard. She had just recently married her college boyfriend. Shelley was raised in Pennsylvania, grew up Christian with no heat in her house, with her mom nurturing stray women and cooking tuna noodle casseroles.

Shelley and I were instant kindred spirits. Twenty years later she is still my best friend. Shelley kept me alive during the worst of my depression. She and my mom. We share a love of music, theater, ideas, talking, and people. We type everyone we know with Myers Briggs. Because she is taller than me, in order to meet my face at eye level, she splayed her legs out wide to make herself six inches shorter while we talked that first day. I laughed out loud because she looked so silly doing that. But she did that for me, and I loved her for it.

Shelley and I started meeting for lunch when we realized we were both working in downtown DC. During those lunches we primarily talked about the church. Shelley was not new to church life since she'd grown up Christian, but she was new to this church and even for her it seemed intense.

Over sandwiches, we talked about everything we were seeing and experiencing. The intensity and passion. The dynamics of hierarchy we both felt on the music team. We wondered why all the women who were a little bit older than us seemed to follow the same pattern: get married, get pregnant, quit their jobs. Impressive women with good jobs in Washington, DC. Was this what they wanted?

Shelley's parents, seasoned ministry people, were raising concerns whenever she went home to visit. Her dad was concerned the church was too insular. I reasoned that her dad just couldn't see how wonderful it was. Her mother was concerned about how the church wrote off the entire field of modern psychology. Neither of us were on antidepressants then, nor did we imagine ever needing them. A happier duo you never could find. What did we know?

One thing you should know about me is that I don't really do things halfway. When I go in, I go all in. For instance, while I was learning to write this book, but before I really knew how to do it professionally, I needed an effective way to procrastinate, so I took up perfumery. I spent entire days studying the world of fragrances. I learned categories of perfumes such a *citrus floral* and *woodsy musk*, and I learned the names of various perfume houses (the French are known to be the best). I learned the names of plants, oils, and other elements, and words like *chypre*, *vetiver*, *oak moss*, and *civet*. I learned the names of perfumers and the names of the people who dated the perfumers and the names of perfumers' godchildren.

As you might imagine, Shelley and I both went all in.

doors.

WHEN I THINK of what a church should be I think of peace. I think of stillness. I think of acceptance and love. I think of a place where you can go to be alone to pray and feel connected to something bigger than yourself. I also think of doors.

It should have been a warning sign that the church only had doors leading in. I don't mean literally, obviously—the church had physical doors. In theory I could have left at any time, but it didn't feel that way. Once you were in, there was always more you could do, more you could learn, ways to be better. I am guessing that ordinary churches do not attempt to catch you and keep you there indefinitely. Therefore, they also do not attempt to replace everyone else in society you could possibly need, such as your family, your school, your marriage counselor, your doctor, your sex therapist, your activities director, your parents, your police department, your mental health professional, and your God. But then again, I had never attended an ordinary church for any length of time.

Care Groups were smaller groups that met in people's homes and were a significant part of church life. You'd show up, eat cookies, pray for each other, discuss Bible verses. They made a large church feel small, and if you wanted any real connection in the church you would want to be in one.

Anything about your personal life, marriage, children, parenting, or spiritual life was up for discussion at Care Group. You got in deep, and you got in quick. You never knew exactly what was going to happen. Sometimes you left feeling encouraged and wonderful, other times embarrassed and exposed. They could put you in a vulnerable spot in front of others. But never right at first.

It was common for a new person to be invited to visit a Care Group. It was a brilliant retention tactic actually, because a person couldn't officially join a Care Group until becoming a member, and they couldn't become a member until they took a ten-week course and agreed in writing to what they had learned. People just wanted to get to the fun stuff, so it was easy to be all *ya ya I agree* and miss the fine print, which was straight out of Rumpelstiltskin: *spin all this straw into gold by morning or else give up your firstborn child.*

Once you completed the course on the church doctrine, the next step was to go for a new member's interview with a pastor. There you'd need to tell your story, and the pastors had to be satisfied that you were a "real Christian," because there were so many counterfeits these days, they said. If you made it this far then you were in, but not until you agreed to do two things: attend a small group regularly and commit to a volunteer team. Oh, and agree to be put under church discipline if necessary.

If you jumped through all these hoops, then you could sign on the dotted line and finally become an official member of the *greatest place on Earth.* Yay!

saved.

NOW THAT I think about it, I got "saved" on the premise of shame. It is such an awful feeling, shame. It is no wonder that it works so well to effect change on a person.

I got the message pretty quick that sex was terrible and something that was only supposed to happen in marriage. I'd come in as quite the disappointing creature since I'd lost my virginity already. I was also enlightened to the fact that my body never actually belonged to me. It belonged to God *and* my future husband. By having sex before I got married, I had actually stolen my own body out from under its true owners!

I always thought sex was just a normal part of growing up, but came to find out all this time I had been doing something wrong and, worse, God had been watching me? (Ew.) And now there was nothing I could do to change this. I had no choice but try to make it up to God.

The night I was feeling awful and terrible about all of this was the night I decided to give my life to God. I got down on my knees and apologized for using my body selfishly and for ruining my special gift of innocence that was supposed to have been for my future husband. My poor future husband! I cried a bunch, though I'm honestly not sure if I truly actually felt terrible or I just thought I *should* feel terrible. I also wasn't sure how sorry a person needed to be in this case, but I did the best I could. In exchange for my awful deeds, I promised God my devotion.

Then I opened up my Bible with my eyes closed. I slipped my finger in (so that God could choose the page), and I chose a spot for my finger to land on. I opened my eyes to see my fortune. I think it was Jeremiah 29:11, "For I know the plans I have for you," but I can't tell you for sure because I threw that Bible away a few years ago along with all of my church books and a banker's box of sermon notes. I kept only a few books so that when I wrote this story I could remember all the crazy stuff I used to believe.

the heart is deceitful.

MY MOTHER AND I have a lot of conversations these days about women and why we ignore our own knowing. It's easy now to see the precise moments I should have trusted my gut. But things were not so black and white then as they are to me now.

She ignored her own wisdom and her mother's advice about her marriage, despite having that knowing feeling inside that her marriage to my father probably wasn't the right thing for her. She went and did it anyway like many brides do—the truth getting lost in the business of flowers and gowns and cakes. Or fear of the unknown. Or other people's wishes. Or the millions of other reasons truth gets lost.

By the time my mother had me she was better acquainted with herself, and so she taught me early about this magical thing, my knowing. She called it intuition or the little voice inside me. Or she'd say to follow my heart. I am lucky I had parents who never told me who to be. Even as a tiny kid they respected me as someone who could make choices for herself. I got the message from them loud and clear that I was my own person and I made the decisions for me.

The rules of life were different at the church, though. Here, God made things happen. Men made things happen. And women? Well, women waited. You weren't supposed to trust your heart here, you were supposed to *distrust* it. That went for everyone, but especially for women and children. Here God, leaders, authorities were for trusting. Just thinking about it I can almost feel my independence and autonomy being pulled out from under me as the responsibility for my life shifted to others. Everyone had someone above them telling them what to do or what God wanted. Children had parents, single men and women had small-group leaders, small-group leaders had pastors, married women had husbands *and* pastors.

On top of this, the Bible itself was presented as a complicated book requiring expert knowledge to truly understand. (I failed to ask why only one of our leaders had a degree in theology). The one thing that was supposed to provide clarity for my life was presented as if understanding was *just outside* my reach, which meant placing even more trust in the leaders of the church.

In theory, it all sounded fine. But the reality was that I did feel the ground shift beneath my feet. People were telling me what I should think, do, and feel. I no longer felt the freedom to have the answers for myself. There wasn't any following my heart. There was only follow the leader. So I adjusted the way people do in new environments. I observed the people around me to get my cues. I figured I had a lot to learn. The question constantly dangling in the forefront of my mind: *Am I doing this right?*

I felt like a child going through that stage from innocence to adolescence—that time when they are like quiet sponges soaking up everything they are hearing and seeing as they try so hard to make sense of the world. The carefree spirit disappears, they retreat into their minds, and you can practically see them sorting and filing everything they are absorbing. They want to know what they know and what they don't, so they won't have to feel silly for not knowing.

the audition.

AS I MENTIONED, every member of the church was required to do two things: join a Care Group and volunteer on one of the teams to keep the church running on mostly unpaid labor. Naturally, I tried out for the music team.

I had been put in touch with a musician named Steve, and it was arranged for us to meet one evening for an audition. When I arrived that evening the auditorium was dimly lit and empty except for Steve, who was on the stage sitting in front of a keyboard waiting for me.

Steve was kind, easygoing, no stress. Buttery radio voice. One hundred percent likable by anyone. He had asked me to bring a song to sing, so I had prepared a verse and a chorus of "Amazing Grace," acapella. He tested my ability to match pitch, checked my range, and then invited me onto the team right then and there. All was fine until he started in on a bit that sounded sort of like mommy talk for grown-ups. *Being on the worship team was a privilege . . . a significant responsibility . . . representing the leadership . . . people will be looking to you.*

I drifted off while Steve talked, thinking that his words felt heavy and stilted, and wondered why they sounded like they were coming from someone else. When he finished he asked me if I understood. *People learn to worship from watching the worship team. I could be removed. Modest dress.*

"I understand," I said. But I didn't really.

I heard the subtext behind Steve's words, but I hadn't been at the church long enough to really understand it. It was the expectation that would be laid out for just about any visible leadership position in the church. And I did not understand just how rare a thing it was for a woman to be given one. These kinds of speeches elevated the significance of the position beyond what it really was. They wanted you to think you were getting this great privilege and honor so in exchange they could exercise more control over you.

the recording session.

THE CHURCH JUST happened to be launching a new music label at the time I arrived on the scene and the energy around everything musical was high. Soon after I started working with the worship team, Steve informed me they were making a live worship album for the label and asked if I could sing on it. I saw the opportunity as serendipitous. I was thrilled. I decided to delay the move to Nashville by reasoning that I could stay at the church a while and learn the basics of recording.

The night of the recording session I was having a most unfortunate week—I was upset about something (which I don't even remember now), and my emotions were sitting close to the surface. Anything would have made me cry. I thought about canceling the session, but I was new to the music team and it would have been unprofessional.

The session was taking place at Steve's split-level house. When I arrived I was greeted by his wife and their two adorable blonde girls. The microphone was set up in the living room, and power cords were running every which way. When Steve informed me his wife would be assisting him for the evening my heart sank. It should have occurred to me that she would be there. Steve's wife tried to be sweet, but there was no doubt she was working hard to make sure I knew she had seniority over me. She had been micromanaging me since the day I joined the music team, and my anger and frustration had been slowly accumulating. I had been looking forward to this recording session, but her presence suddenly put me on edge.

The two of them headed downstairs to get set up, and I readied myself to sing. I put my headphones on, hummed a little, and we went through a series of sound checks to make sure everyone could hear. Then we started the recording. I was in the middle of singing the first phrase when Steve's wife interrupted me with a note of correction. Then I began again. I started the song a second time and sang another phrase or two when she interrupted me again. I was not in the mood for this and wasn't dealing well. When it happened a third time I couldn't blow up in anger, so instead I started to cry.

I was so embarrassed that I had disrupted the session. They both came upstairs to check in with me, and we headed up to the kitchen for a short break. She made me some tea, and her demeanor toward me softened. About ten minutes later we all went back downstairs to finish the recording.

That night I went home happy with my work, except for the crying. I tried to console myself with the thought that it is the emotions lying close to the surface that help artists bring music alive for people who prefer balancing checkbooks and equations for fun. I was mortified, but my emotions had betrayed me throughout my life more times than I could count. It was just another day in the life.

The next day Bob, the head of music, asked me to come to his office. I was a little wary because the last time I was in Bob's office I was told I was taking too much initiative. But I was hopeful that he just wanted to say something positive about my vocal work or thank me for volunteering my time. Instead he interrogated me about the recording session and the crying.

I would have preferred to tell him the truth—that Steve's wife had been hard at work establishing hierarchy between us and I wasn't appreciating it. But instead I gave a vague answer, saying it was personal. Bob responded with a threat that caught me off guard. He said, "If anything like this ever happens again you will never record for Sovereign Grace again." For the record, this would have been absolutely understandable if I was being treated like a professional. Or paid like a professional. But I wasn't. I was volunteering my time and talents. I bolted out of his office as fast as I could, extremely unsettled.

It was a strange feeling. Out in the world I was successful. I felt bright and voluminous and happy. People loved working with me. I was treated with respect. But here I felt small, ungrounded, and somehow always wrong. One day I'd realize that is exactly what I should have been feeling, because in this place, all I had to do to be wrong was wake up in the morning.

> *The original sin of being born female is not redeemable by works.*
>
> Anne Wilson Shaef

• • •

We betray ourselves because we believe we are getting something good in exchange for that act of betrayal. I thought that getting to sing with these people was a great opportunity. Working with someone as talented as Bob was a genuine opportunity and I knew it. But it was never worth trading my personal integrity for.

We make trades like this for different reasons. For ease. For ambition. For the sake of another person. For lack of courage. For an escape. We underestimate the impact one decision in our lives can make in directing the rest of it. We underestimate the impact of small, tiny decisions that build up over time. We imagine what we are getting for our compromise is far better than it really is. And we underestimate the cost to ourselves.

When we don't speak on our own behalf it is like inviting the world to relate to a false version of ourselves. If you pretend something doesn't matter when actually it does you're essentially lying to yourself and whomever you are relating to. Then people get used to this version of you who is lying and they come to expect this false you. Even you get used to this false you. And in this way you can get stuck in it, just like getting caught in a lie. You cannot lie to the world and expect to get truth back.

But when we are true to ourselves it forces the world to reckon with the real us. People have to respond to the real us, which in turn gives us a better chance of seeing the real them.

I often think about what would have happened that day if I had told the truth in Bob's office, because I know what would have happened. I would have gotten kicked off the music team. Which would have freed me to focus on fulfilling my actual dreams for my life instead of the church's dreams for my life.

the ambush.

THE CHURCH TAUGHT that the roles of men and women in marriage were a beautiful thing, and I believed them. They said that women were equal in worth but separate in function. Men were *called to the work* and women were called to *help* with the work. They said this was so because in Genesis God gave Adam the job of naming the animals but gave Eve the job of helping Adam. This was proof, they said, that women are here on earth *to help.*

Also, they said it was because Eve was made from Adam's rib, so this meant she was literally made from a man and thus never her own to begin with.

And just in case there was any doubt, we were reminded that Eve was easily deceived when she gave in to temptation and took the apple, so clearly she needed a leader.

And if that still wasn't enough they said that Eve acted as a temptress when she offered the apple to Adam, and sadly, that is why she and all future women are at fault for the fall of *all mankind.*

I don't know about you, but when I read these statements and put the ideas they convey into my own words, I hear women being called some disrespectful names:

"different"
"subordinate"
"useful for reproduction"
"secondary"
"less intelligent"
"bad influence"
"the one who failed"

So let's get this straight. These theologians somehow convinced me that the purpose of a woman has nothing to do with who she was born to be, but who some mystery man in her future was born to be?

And Eve is ultimately responsible for all the bad things that happen in the world?

And that Adam would have been fine by himself, but "*that thar* woman" led him into sin?

Do you know what this sounds like to me now?

It sounds like a freaking *ambush.*

equal in worth.

WHEN I CAME into the church I didn't understand conservative Christian culture. I didn't know its history or realize I'd just dropped in at a fairly significant point in the timeline. Conservative evangelicals had been feeling increasingly threatened by the feminist movement and claimed that marriage and the family were under siege. They suggested that women were getting out of control, losing their vision for womanhood, deserting their families for careers, and usurping male leadership. Evangelicals responded to feminism by bolstering their message and digging their heels in further on the issue of female submission, and they called upon women to save the day. Women would save Christian families by following the teachings of the church and embracing their God-given role as supporters and helpers. Women should ignore the social inequalities that were being touted by feminists.

The pastors and theologians selling submission were sneaky, and they had to be because submission only works if you can get women to agree to it. They formed a council, wrote a new Bible translation, and found ways of talking about submission that made it sound noble and beautiful, taking advantage of the protective spirit and sense of duty and loyalty that many women naturally have.

• • •

I wanted to believe what the church was telling me because I never wanted to have to bring my future children into the living room and tell them their family was ending. I thought a church marriage would be safer. I thought the families at church looked happy. Their kids were smiling. The parents were smiling. I wanted a happy, smiling family too. I thought following these rules would give me back the things I'd lost as a child. I thought it would not, it could not fail.

The language used to soften the sound of submission to a woman's ears is clever. We were told women were equal to men in worth—only the roles were different. We were told women were honored and respected. Leaders were not to be leader lords but servant leaders. Husbands were taught they should "love their wives as their own bodies," nourishing and cherishing them as they would for themselves.

In a well-crafted sermon, this can almost sound fine. The problem is that people live in the real world, where things are definitely not always fine and the conservative evangelical answer to this problem is to pretend it doesn't exist. Which begs the question: What happens when things are *not fine*? What happens when a woman trades her autonomy, her body, her intuition, her career, her dreams, her choices and preferences in return for protection, honoring, and cherishing, but then on the other side of her marriage vows she isn't actually protected, honored, or cherished? What does she do then?

Hierarchy creates order, and I get that this can be comforting and even helpful in certain situations like hospitals and the military. There is a time and a place for leaders and followers. But not inside a person's most intimate relationship, on which the bulk of a person's happiness, mental health, and well-being rests. Not unless there's a way out of *worse*. Because let's think about *worse* for a second. When I got married, I vowed to love for better or for worse, and my only thought of *worse* was cancer. Of course, I would stick it out for *that* worse.

But what if worse is a husband who enjoys forcing his wife to do sex acts she doesn't want to do? What if worse is the husband loses his job and decides it's easier to become a drug addict than to reinvent himself? What if worse is beatings? Controlling food? Sexual assault? Abusive words? Emotional manipulation? Abandonment? Neglect? Abusing the kids? What if worse is constant criticism? Years of disinterest? This is the man who promised to protect and cherish? To love and honor and treat his wife's body as his own?

See, I think the inventors of submission forgot to give *worse* the thought it deserves. Which is interesting, since these are the same people who teach the theology that humans are only full of sin and nothing else. Let's be clear. It's not the marriages that are thriving that reveal the fine print of inequality and lack of respect for women inherent in this structure. It's the marriages where *worse* is happening. Because there is an enormous difference between caring for a sick husband *worse* and being disrespected or harmed *worse*. And yet, in either case, the church expects nearly the same exact thing of women: love unconditionally, irrevocably, unquestionably, forever.

In my fifteen-plus years of ministry I am not certain that a woman at my church, under the leadership of my pastor, would have been supported in leaving her husband for any reason. Not for physical abuse. Not for sexual abuse. Not for emotional abuse, neglect, financial abuse, cruelty, not even for child abuse, God help us all.

• • •

I've learned a lot of things since then. I have learned that families breaking can be healthy. That nothing in life is safe. I've learned not to trust men who have all the answers or have stopped being curious. I've learned that the families who are always smiling are often the ones hurting the most. And I've learned that women are some of the most invisible, resilient, exploited, beautiful creatures on the planet.

love.

THE FIRST TIME I took notice of my future husband Joshua, he was on a speaking tour. He had just arrived from Oregon, and a group of us twentysomethings from the church went to hear him speak. I was taken with his charm and humor, his gorgeous dark eyes and almost black wavy hair.

He was the oldest child in a family of seven. His parents had been early pioneers of the homeschooling movement, and his family was well-known in Christian homeschooling circles. As a teenager he created a magazine for Christian teens that was read by thousands across the country. This led to further opportunities for speaking engagements and conference tours.

CJ's teenage daughters were subscribers to the magazine, and it was through them that CJ first became aware of Josh. When CJ hosted a conference for young men considering a vocation in ministry, he invited Josh to attend. Around this same time, Josh was in the final stages of writing a book about sexual purity.

At the conference, CJ was intentional about pursuing him, persuading him to enter the ministry on the basis of his charisma and gift for public speaking. He suggested to Josh that he was a "Timothy" in need of a "Paul," meaning a young man who needed an older mentor. He offered himself as that mentor and invited Josh to come live with him and his family in their home.

• • •

I was standing next to Josh when the first shipment of his printed books was delivered. He picked a book out of the box and showed it to me. *I Kissed Dating Goodbye.* I thought it was a catchy title. It was a book on Christian romance and dating. Or not dating, actually. *Courtship* was the term he used. Courtship was supposedly more purposeful and less experimental than dating, more like a first step toward marriage, only with no sex. I flipped it over to the back. There was a sepia-toned photo of Josh with some serious puppy dog eyes. He signed the copy and handed it to me. It was 1997.

The purity movement was already well established by this time, but Josh's book would raise the obsession with chastity to a whole new level among conservative evangelicals. The movement started in the early 1990s in reaction to the 1960–70s era of free love and the threat of the AIDS virus in the 1980s. In 1993, Southern Baptists held the first True Love Waits campaign, where more than two hundred thousand teens stood on the National Mall signing pledges of abstinence. Purity balls, purity rings, purity pledges abounded. Even Miley Cyrus and Selena Gomez had purity rings at one point. The rings symbolized a commitment to abstain from sex until marriage.

I Kissed Dating Goodbye turned *courtship* into a buzzword and Josh into a kind of abstinence pop star. The book was extremely popular with parents and churches. It provided a strong message and a handsome kid to communicate it. It offered a formula for Christian romance that seemed too good to be true. And for many it was.

• • •

While courtship may have led some young people to a happy union, for others it wasn't so simple. This was a culture highly fixated on performance and perfection. Purity often became more important than the relationship itself. The potential for relationships to be pushed straight to marriage in order to avoid physical "mishaps" was high. There were risks of marrying without having sufficient time to explore compatibility. Risks of marrying too young. And it was easy for authority figures to involve themselves too much in the process, playing both God and matchmaker.

There were other problems too. Immature boys were under tremendous pressure to be leaders, and immature girls were under pressure to be followers. Boys were supposed to "hear from God," and girls were supposed to hope they heard right. Young women were especially at risk of not having the final say in the choice of a spouse, their voice in the matter getting buried under a parent, pastor, or suitor. Many young people were at risk of committing to unions for life that were not well suited for them, or for the wrong reasons.

As for my own thoughts about courtship, it was a clear picture of the two versions of me living inside me. I had one foot in my old life and one in the new. Part of me felt lighthearted about it, almost patronizing. I thought it was "cute." On the other hand the church was telling me that my lack of virginity was cause for shame, and I saw it as a chance for me to do things differently. It's also possible that I had romanticized courtship in my mind a bit. And if I hadn't done that, Jane Austen would have been doing it for me. BBC's *Pride and Prejudice* came out in 1995 and *Emma* in 1996, and both romanticized the heck out of courtship. I figured it worked out well enough for Elizabeth and Darcy.

A year later, when Josh asked me to start a relationship with him, I'd already quietly liked him for a year. I'd taken a temporary job working for the church, and I saw him several times a week when he wasn't traveling. There were plenty of "signs" that he was the one. I took no initiative (unless you count making my eyes twinkle on purpose and employing other invisible feminine powers I carried deep within me). I also prayed like mad. Girls were allowed to do that.

• • •

Because of Josh's book, his audience, and his new official position at the church, both he and CJ felt Josh could not afford to make any mistakes in the relationship. Even a small amount of physical activity would have been perceived as weakness and failure. The solution was to have no physical activity, except for hand-holding and the occasional hug. This extra-strict code of conduct was above and beyond what Josh was suggesting in his book, but Christian America likes its leaders to be demi-gods, and they like to play along.

I highly doubt many of the parents and pastors pushing courtship had ever tried it themselves. They likely found their spouses the old-fashioned way. Flirting, dates, and trying not to go all the way but maybe doing it anyway. I went along with it not because I agreed it was necessary, but because I was in love with him. But there were a number of problems with our courtship. And perhaps none greater than the fact that the moment it started it stopped being about us.

fishbowl.

THE FIRST SUNDAY I went to church after my courtship began, I walked into the auditorium feeling about as inconspicuous as a whale on a beach. Despite the church size being roughly a thousand people, news spread quickly, and I could feel it in the air. I came in late and therefore took the first empty seat I found. No one I knew was sitting nearby.

Suffice it to say it had been a crazy week in a crazy place and I was tired. So during worship I had my hands resting in the back pockets of my jeans instead of raising my hands in the usual passionate way that people did during the singing. Because I'm human and my arms were tired and because they were *my* arms.

The service ended and before I finished collecting my things to leave, the woman sitting behind me tapped me on the shoulder and proceeded to ask me if she could talk to me a moment. It sounded very grave, so of course I said yes—but if this ever happens to you, just tell the person you don't have any moments. It was the hands in the jeans, of course. I wasn't worshipping "good enough" now that I was in a relationship with the youth pastor. I needed to be an example now, she said. All the young people would be watching me.

Confrontations like these were a hallmark of the church culture. They were reframed as love or helping someone grow. The church called them *observations.* But they were also a control tactic and method of gauging a person's willingness to conform. If you didn't receive someone's observation well, you might be labeled unteachable or worse. And if you were unteachable or worse you definitely wouldn't be promoted to a leadership role or get to play Mary in the Christmas pageant. With this whole rigmarole, the church found a way to reward and promote those who would conform. For me, even the smallest, most ordinary moments of my life began to feel like performances to be evaluated.

flowers, cherries, and apples.

WHEN I ARRIVED at the front door of the Mahaneys' home, I took a minute to calm my nerves. I looked at the modest, neatly trimmed shrubs to the left of the door. Then I looked down at my outfit and decided it was stupid. I was already sweating even though it was winter. It wasn't the first time I was meeting them, but it was the first time I was meeting them as the the potential wife of their future leader. With Josh's parents three thousand miles away in Oregon, it would be the Mahaneys' fault if he accidentally married an axe murderer. Since I no longer had my virginity, I was dangerously close to that.

I knocked, and Carolyn opened the door. She smiled and greeted me warmly. From watching her on Sundays, I'd guessed that Carolyn wasn't really energized by social interaction, but she was trying to make me feel welcome. Josh, a few of the Mahaneys' daughters, and I made small talk in the kitchen while Carolyn finished the dinner preparations. CJ was not home yet from work and arrived just in time for the dinner.

Carolyn, with her Florida Mennonite background, made a delicious dinner of ham, green bean casserole, and homemade cottage cheese rolls. I was relieved when we sat down to dinner so I could have a rest from all the attention. It was obvious CJ and Carolyn were assessing my suitability as a potential partner for Josh. CJ had a particularly keen interest in who would be joining his royal court. He needed to make sure the woman Josh chose would uphold the values of the church.

When dessert was served and conversation winding down, CJ asked me to sing something. I laughed uncomfortably and said,

"No thank you," but then went ahead and did it because I hadn't yet learned to believe in my no.

After dinner we moved into the living room. Whenever I was around CJ it was impossible not to notice his energy, his posture. He was intense, with something always bubbling just under the surface. When he preached, one leg would often be slightly forward and diagonal, and he'd rock back and forth while he spoke. This night CJ was sitting in a chair but on the edge, leaning forward, with his bald, Irish head jutting out so far it appeared almost turtle-like.

He started in with what seemed to be "getting to know you" questions. What was the story of my faith? When did I first start liking Josh? Where did my parents live? Were they divorced? Had I gone to public school?

As I answered, CJ's forward-projecting intensity did nothing to help me know him or feel at ease. His posture let me know this was not a two-way relationship. He was the driver. Always the driver.

The questions moved toward my past relationships. Tell us about your previous boyfriends? It felt like CJ was moving a thin, sharp needle closer and closer to my skin. *OK, I know where this is headed.* Virginity. Or in my case, lost virginity. My emotions began to rise again like a pressure cooker building up steam.

Now of course I can see that all of the questions pointed to ways I fell short of their ideal. My secular background, public school, divorced parents, lost virginity. I came from the outside world these people worked so hard to avoid. It didn't matter that my parents were both wonderful people, or that I had been a high-achieving, responsible person basically since birth. They could not see past their ideals. Their perception of me was colored almost entirely by the state of my virginity. It didn't even matter that Josh himself hadn't been completely chaste. His sexual history wasn't up for discussion. The double standard was alive and well. Because of me, Josh wouldn't get his innocent virgin bride, and someone needed to account for that.

I really don't think anyone in the room truly cared that I wasn't a virgin. It seemed like what everybody wanted was just to make sure I knew that I had failed in their eyes.

I answered their questions but not without feeling exposed and invaded and disrespected. When the pressure finally reached the limit, I started to cry. I could tell they thought my tears were because I was ashamed, and I let them think that, but that wasn't it. I loved my childhood. I wasn't ashamed of my adolescence.

Still, I did feel a powerful sense of shame. Now I realize that it wasn't my own shame that I was feeling, it was their shame about me that I felt and it cut deep that day. No one had ever gone out of their way before to tell me I was bad. I didn't have any tools for dealing with this. I just believed it.

I was a young, talented woman, full of energy and life and anticipation for my future. But my honeymoon period with the church was over. Now it felt like I was being punished and handed heavy bricks. First the brick that I had disappointed God by losing my virginity and damaging my future marriage before it had even started. Then another brick that I was inherently evil and no good came from within me. And another brick that I was the weaker sex. And then another brick that my body and my life didn't belong to me. Those were heavy bricks the church handed women to carry. Is it any wonder some of us get tired?

The church applied Eve's sin to all women, all the time. We all had to carry it because of her. That was our cross to bear. She sinned, therefore so had we. We were the lesser sex. We took the fruit. We failed.

So there we were. In one hand holding this great sacrifice and in the other hand holding an apple.

ten weeks.

MY FIRST KISS was after morning kindergarten under a sleeping bag at Mark's house. (Mark's mom was in the kitchen making us a snack.) When I was eight or nine I was taking a bubble bath with my friend, and her *very* older sister came in and told us to let the water run between our legs and see how long we could stand it. When I was thirteen, I found *The Joy of Sex* on my mom's bookshelf and closed it promptly when I saw a drawing of a man sucking on a woman's armpit. *Gross.* In high school I lost my virginity. In college I had real sex.

And here I was twenty-five years old and barely touching someone I might possibly marry and thinking somehow that this made sense. My God, we were all so much in our minds that our bodies were levitating. No one's feet were touching the ground—we were *that* holy. Whose ideas were these rules, really?

I had a better sense of personal autonomy *before* coming to the church. Just a few short years earlier I had broken up with my college boyfriend because I realized he felt entitled to my body. That was the end of that. In church, men still felt entitled to my body, only instead of using anger, they used theology to gain control of it. Theology gave men power over my romantic relationships, my body, and even my level of participation in the relationship.

• • •

My relationship with Josh was hurried along because a young single man was seen as something of a ticking time bomb. As I mentioned, Josh couldn't afford to make any mistakes because he'd just written his book on doing Christian romance "right" and people would be watching. CJ couldn't afford for Josh to make any mistakes because he wanted Josh to be the model to which he could point other young men. We all rallied around Josh to help make sure he lived up to these expectations.

I was getting updates on how *my* relationship was going through Josh, who unbeknownst to me was getting them from CJ. I saw Josh as an independent, capable young man who had been working for the past four years running a magazine and conferences on his own. I had no idea how much Josh was being influenced and infantilized by CJ. "It's going to be a long courtship and a short engagement," Josh told me at first. A little while later the plan was reversed.

Other couples were getting bad relationship advice. One woman who was having doubts about marrying was told that attraction to her potential husband wasn't important; she just needed to ask herself if she could follow the man. Keeping relationships chaste was such a focus that attraction and physical chemistry were hardly discussed until engagement. At this point, I had done more in a sleeping bag with Mark from morning kindergarten than my twenty-four-year-old adult boyfriend.

• • •

One day at Starbucks Carolyn sat me down to tell me that if I moved forward in marrying Josh I would have to give up my dreams. She wanted to be sure I knew I was signing up for a life of sacrifice, and assured me it wouldn't be an easy life. She asked me if I was prepared for that. I suppose I have to give credit where credit is due. She did try to warn me.

I have never forgotten that moment. I can still picture her face when she said it wouldn't be an easy life. I thought I caught a glimpse of something in Carolyn's eyes that I had never seen before, nor would I afterward. A glimpse of sadness, maybe. Was there some feeling behind this stoic woman after all? Maybe being married to CJ, being the queen of his kingdom, was harder for her than I knew. I wondered for a moment what dreams she may have had.

I also thought she was crazy. Did she have no imagination? For me? For herself? Why did she assume I would live my life exactly like her? I was not the same person as Carolyn. *I would never give up on my dreams. Never.*

Why was she describing for me a house with no windows or doors? A life with no inspiration? Why did Carolyn rarely laugh? What kind of woman would hold out the death of a dream for another woman to grab hold of? And what woman in her right mind would say yes to that?

• • •

Ten weeks after our relationship began, Josh and I flew out to meet his family. I understood the trip to be about getting to know them better and vice versa. *Long courtship* was the last thing I'd heard. To my surprise, he asked me to marry him on that trip. Happily, I said yes.

it will be fine.

IT WAS MY first conference as Josh's significant other. Josh wanted me to join him on his speaking tours now that we were engaged, so I quit my job so that I could travel with him. I'd taken an administrative job at the church, and I could think of nothing I'd rather do less than data entry, making charts, and trying to remember things other people were doing two weeks from now.

It was the end of the day, after Josh had delivered at least three talks. We'd arrived at the moment where everyone wanted to meet him or have him sign their book or snap a picture. I was sitting in the front row, where I had been the whole conference. From the front of the stage our eyes met, and he motioned for me to come up and stand next to him. When I did I turned and saw the line of people, mostly girls, that went from us to Costa Rica. *This is going to take a while.*

Girl after girl came up to hug him, take a picture with him, talk with him. Their eyes lit up when it was their turn. He was their hero, and they loved it and he loved it. I looked on amazed as the hours went by and from the first to the last person his energy level hardly waned. The girls just wanted to have their chance to talk and touch their star. They wanted to be seen.

I learned a lot from these young girls who were eager to talk about their world. It was a crash course in Homeschooling Families 101. The conferences Josh gave were centered around the topics in his book, which meant romance, so naturally most girls wanted to talk about their love life. The girls I met fit into four categories. Girls who were sad because they were trying to adopt this higher standard of purity and it wasn't easy. Girls who believed they'd already failed in some way and were feeling terribly ashamed. Girls who were angry because their parents were demanding they end a relationship or would not allow them to date. Girls who were choosing to wait for their dream man to come along at just the right time.

By the time Josh hugged and listened to the last girl, I was spent. My face muscles hurt from smiling so much. It had been more than two hours. Standing next to Josh all that time had me thinking. I was proud of him and proud to be with him, but I couldn't help but wonder. Why was I here? How was I helping anyone? After all, as a woman and a wife, "helping" would be my official job description. Clearly, he had this well under control. Wouldn't it be a better use of my time to be doing something related to my gifts and talents rather than standing here smiling and nodding? I heaved a sigh, but reasoned with myself. This was just one day, one scenario. We had a whole life ahead of us. *It will be fine.*

mint pies.

CAROLYN WAS GOING to start formally mentoring me for my upcoming role as a pastor's wife. I loved a good challenge, and I was ready to do something more. I assumed I would gradually take on more responsibility until I became the senior pastor's wife. The senior pastors' wives in our denomination were typically responsible for directing the women's ministry, teaching women, overseeing an administrative team, developing relationships with other pastors' wives in the community and beyond, hosting and entertaining constantly, and most of all, keeping their husbands infinitely satisfied and their children on the straight and narrow. I figured there was a lot to cover between now and then. But my hopes were quickly dashed once we started because I sensed she was only mentoring me out of obligation. I suspected as much for three reasons. One, I didn't think she liked doing it. Two, I didn't like doing it either. And three, we didn't talk about any of those responsibilities.

Every couple of weeks she would pick me up perfectly punctually and we would drive to one of the three nearby Starbucks. I always felt anxious while I was waiting for Carolyn to arrive. I didn't feel at ease, and I found it difficult to make a connection with her. We were not peers, we were not friends, and Carolyn wasn't open to sharing personally with me. It was not uncommon for me to drum up things ahead of time to be "struggling with" to make sure we could keep the conversation flowing. We'd sit there for an hour. I'd jot down things she said in a notebook.

We had no official agenda, and generally we only talked about husbands, children, or managing the home. Items that could immediately be connected to Titus 2:3–5, Carolyn's life verses: "Likewise, teach the older women to be reverent in the way they live, not to be slanderers or addicted to much wine, but to teach what is good. Then they can urge the younger women to love their husbands and children, to be self-controlled and pure, to be busy at home, to be kind, and to be subject to their husbands, so that no one will malign the word of God" (NIV). It is what she taught the women of the church and what she lived at home. She never stepped outside of this material that I recall, God bless her soul.

The thing about mentors is this. They should want to mentor you, or at least get paid to mentor you. Carolyn was doing it because she had to. And whatever "it" was, it definitely wasn't mentoring. We never talked about ways that I could expand. We never talked about my past or my future. We didn't discuss how best to utilize my gifts for the women's ministry. I cannot see how we were aiming for anything in those meetings that would benefit me. What the mentorship did do, however, was provide a context for her to confront me if she didn't like what I was doing. And it gave CJ an inside reach to Josh and me. Carolyn could be his eyes and ears as well as his voice if needed.

Once, instead of meeting at Starbucks she asked me come to her home. She had an especially busy week and needed to do some cooking, and so we would spend our time in her kitchen instead. I remember thinking her house looked a lot like her. Serious, orderly, and a bit austere with a hint of attempting to be warm. Perhaps a reflection of her Mennonite background. She took me down to the basement, where they had remodeled to make room for Josh and another Pastor's College student. Peeking in the laundry room, there was not one stray sock or basket visible, or even a jar for coins or any of the clutter most people have in their homes.

She took me out to her garage, where she kept a large chest freezer. She lifted the lid and we both leaned forward, peering in. She showed me all the meals she had prepared and stored in large Ziplock bags labeled in black Sharpie pen. *Chicken Kiev. Chocolate mint pies.* For unexpectedly busy days or last-minute guests. I remember staring down at her perfectly stocked freezer and thinking, *I am not this person.*

This is Carolyn's womanhood. This is not my womanhood. Carolyn closed the lid and we went back to the kitchen.

Maybe it was that day, or perhaps another one. But at some point she handed me a mixing bowl with some chocolate Rice Krispies in it and a glass measuring cup with melted mint chocolate. She wanted me to help her make one of her chocolate mint pies. The ones that were in the freezer.

"Here, you can stir this," she said.

I looked down at the gooey mixture of chocolate and Rice Krispies in the stainless-steel bowl. I was beginning to wonder if I would ever have a real, meaningful role in this church.

the ring.

I WORE A ring on my right hand. It was a simple thin gold band. It was given to me by my high school boyfriend, James. I think he may have wanted to marry me and was hoping it might strengthen our relationship before I left for college, but I just wasn't ready. I offered to give the ring back. He insisted that I keep it. I still wore it simply because I liked the ring. It reminded me of high school—a time when I was thriving and happy, *and* it was one of the few pieces of real jewelry that I owned. I'd never taken the ring off, not since I was a teenager.

One day Josh noticed it on my finger and asked me about it. I was expecting this to come up eventually. I did my best to assuage his fears by explaining to him that James and I had dated during my junior and senior years of high school and that I had broken things off and that I didn't still have feelings and all of that. Still, I wanted to keep the ring.

• • •

I don't think my explanations helped much, because the next thing I knew I was sitting across from Carolyn at a Starbucks and she was asking me about the ring. I was on the spot again and embarrassed to be having to talk to her about this. I started to explain as I had to Josh, but even as the words left my tongue I felt the weight of her disapproval. I made it too easy for her and said out loud the words I knew she was thinking. *I should get rid of the ring.* Her steely blue eyes told me she agreed, but I couldn't help but notice the woman showed less emotion than a refrigerator. I didn't think any of this was necessary, but I wanted to accommodate Josh, who I knew was fearful of the secular culture in which I grew up.

It seemed like Carolyn was going through an awful lot of trouble bringing this up on Josh's behalf, and I thought maybe there was more that she wanted to say. Sure enough, she steered the conversation to my wedding and asked me who I was planning to have as my bridesmaids. I listed off a few friends from church, a relative, and my best girlfriends from home who were not in the church. She proceeded to tell me that my friends *also* made Josh uncomfortable. *My best friends made Josh uncomfortable?* I leaned back in my chair. It was one thing to take off the ring. But these were relationships that were important to me. How could they possibly make him uncomfortable when he'd never even met them?

I slowly took all of this in. Something felt off and strange. I was upset, but I wasn't sure who to be upset with. Was she speaking for Josh or for herself? I could never think straight around Carolyn, but she was waiting for me to say something.

"So, you're saying I can't have my best friends in my own wedding?" I asked, incredulously.

Her answer as usual was crystal clear.

• • •

Josh and I were going to Sanibel Island, Florida, with my family. My grandmother Mums, the photographer-explorer one, wanted to go there to photograph birds and hunt for shells and she had invited some extended family to come along.

For a few weeks I had been thinking about the conversation with Carolyn. On the plane trip down, I made up my mind to keep the ring, but I still needed to tell Josh. One day during the trip we were out playing shuffleboard when I told him. His response was mumbled so I couldn't make out the words, but I didn't need to. I could tell he wasn't happy, and the guilt I felt caught me off guard. I was expecting acceptance or a fight. I wasn't sure what to do with guilt.

Later that afternoon I walked out to the beach alone until my toes hit the edge of the water. Everything about the moment felt wrong. It felt wrong that it should be such a big deal. It felt wrong that Carolyn was the one telling me what to do. It felt wrong that no one acknowledged the ring was important to me, let alone believed my explanation. I knew I was being asked to give up something much more than a ring. I just couldn't see what it was.

I looked out to the horizon feeling confused and misunderstood. I took the ring off my finger and turned it over and over slowly between my fingertips, noticing its delicate smoothness. *It's just a little thing, Shannon, for someone you love. It's just a ring.* Then I pulled my arm back, and as hard as I could I threw my lovely ring into the sea.

royals.

CJ AND CAROLYN were church royalty. And as such they maintained a few degrees of separation between themselves and the commonfolk. I suspect this was something that had originally appealed to CJ about me being the potential wife of his protégé. I didn't come with the type of relational obligations that might have been present if Josh was marrying the daughter of another family in the church.

They encouraged us to separate ourselves from the rest of the church in the same ways that they did. More than a few times I was firmly instructed by Carolyn to keep leadership issues private. I was asked not to share inside information with anyone—not with other members of our pastoral team, not even with my best friend, Shelley. I was encouraged to be cautious about friendships with other pastors' wives too. If anything was clear about what they wanted most from me, it was that they wanted me to keep quiet.

Carolyn believed her own relationships to be dictated by CJ's. If his relationships with men broke down, so did hers with the wives of those men. She held everyone at arm's length, and she suggested that I do the same. I wasn't interested in conducting my relationships in this way. I wanted deep, genuine friendships, and I pursued them and found them. And yet, because of Carolyn's advice, I also unnecessarily isolated myself and my children in certain ways too.

But like they often did, checks in my spirit were swallowed up by the fact that many good things were happening too. Carolyn and CJ were investing time in us. They invited us for dinner numerous times, and Carolyn went above and beyond to make the meals nice. When she found out how much I loved her homemade rolls, she made them again for me. They included us in their family activities at times.

My primary relationships at this time became the pastors' wives, a group of about fifteen women. Most of the women were more than a decade older than me and seasoned. I was new and green. When we weren't traveling our life at home revolved around these relationships. Every month there were meetings. Lots of meetings. There was a meeting for all the pastors and their wives, a meeting for just the wives, a meeting for just the pastors, a meeting for the whole small group, a meeting for just the women of the small group, and a meeting for just the men of the small group. There was also a constant and steady stream of conferences, trainings, and annual events that required our attendance.

There was a lot I didn't understand about my situation, but we were too busy to think. I wasn't looking to find the bad either. It was an exciting time. I was young and embarking on a new adventure. I embraced this world and all that came with it because this happened to be the world of the person I loved.

wedding day.

ONE PHOTOGRAPH FROM my wedding day stands out in my mind. It is a picture of my mother and me. She picked me up early to take me to the hair salon, and my hair turned out badly. I had hired a photographer to follow me around for the day, and he happened to snap a picture of us just at the moment my hair was finished. In the photo we're looking in the mirror and the look on our faces is saying, *This is not looking good*, but we are both trying very hard not to think it. I feel like that photo says it all. My mother, there by my side supporting me, keeping her misgivings to herself, wanting me to be happy. Me, pushing toward a goal, forgetting that if I wanted to I could just reach up to my head and pull all the pins out.

• • •

The ceremony was about to begin, and the church was buzzing with energy. Everyone from the church seemed to be there volunteering. A flock of teenage girls dressed in black and white were helping with the food. They had been released from their duties to watch as I made my entrance. I looked down and saw their faces all giddy with girlish delight.

As my cue got closer, I went to a dimly lit side hallway to wait. My three bridesmaids—my brother's wife and my two closest friends from church—were by my side and we took a minute together. They looked beautiful in their light blue dresses. I took them in, smiling.

Then I looked at the empty space around them where I imagined my childhood and college friends would be. Lauren, Julie, Kathy, Gina, Nikki. For a second, I felt buoyed by a flash of happy memories, but it quickly turned to a sick sense of self-betrayal in my stomach. *These girls that I love are not here with me. How did I let this happen? They were supposed to be here with me.* Then the music changed, and it was time for me to walk in.

• • •

The truth is, it never was *my* wedding. I'd been casually dismissed since we started the planning. I'd wanted the wedding to be in a charming chapel; I was told it needed to be in the church. I wanted to have a dinner reception, but the guest list got so large between my guests, Josh's guests, and Carolyn's and CJ's guests we would have gone above budget. I wanted dancing and alcohol at the reception to celebrate our marriage. That was not even open for discussion. As the wedding drew closer I found myself scrambling to make room for people I wanted there, people I'd left off the list. I even called the mother of a very close friend the day before, sheepishly asking her to attend. Kindly, she did.

My whole family was on the fringes of the activities. I remember seeing my mother and brother there and feeling as though they were foreigners. My mother's involvement in the whole affair had been overshadowed by Josh's real mother, Sono, and my temporary mother, Carolyn. Perhaps it wasn't intentional, but CJ and Carolyn effectively managed to push me to the outside of my own relationship, my own marriage, my own life.

How can I explain the sadness I felt mixed in with the happiness in that moment? I loved this man, and I was happy to be marrying him. But I was betraying so much of myself in the process. As it turned out, I was not really marrying the man I loved. I was marrying the church. And I had not seen that coming.

• • •

When it came time for the pronouncement, CJ was supposed to say *you may now kiss the bride* and be done with it, but instead he took a few minutes to give a mini-sermon on purity and draw everyone's attention to the fact that we had waited until this day to have our first kiss. I did not know he was planning to do this, and I was both mortified and angry at him for it. It hit me right then and there that in all the plans for the wedding CJ had not once considered me. He hadn't considered how uncomfortable that might make my guests feel. Or the fact that this was my event and most of my personal guests were not from the church. I invited them there to share in my wedding day, not to receive an evangelistic or moral sales pitch.

Just as I turned to face my guests as the *New Mrs. Harris,* I was angry and full of mixed emotions, but I forced a smile so my guests would feel happy. And when my eyes teared up, I let them think my tears were from happiness, but they weren't.

ménage à trois and me.

OUR MARRIAGE NEVER stood a chance if forever is the only measure of success one is willing to use. It was doomed to fail from the beginning for a number of reasons. Any one of them would have been enough to destroy a marriage.

What I can tell you is that it was crowded on the stage where I gave my vows. The man I chose was already betrothed to an audience and a pastor. Our relationship was subservient to those two relationships, and unfortunately, it remained that way throughout our marriage. This wasn't a situation of two human beings joined in matrimony to create a life together, based on mutual respect and desire to invest time, resources, and energy into building the relationship. It wasn't even a situation where two people met and fell in love. It was a situation where a man and his pastor decided it was time to get married, and they both had something to gain by his marrying me.

CJ exerted undue influence in every single area of his young protégé's life at this time. He convinced my husband to go into the ministry when he wasn't certain that was what he wanted. He convinced him he needed a mentor. He convinced him to move into his home with him. He convinced him to put a thriving, independent ministry under his control. Can I honestly expect he didn't also exert too much influence in the timing of his marriage or the choice of his bride?

And about that bride. I wish I could have seen that I was not respected, or accepted as the real, whole me. Not by the church or my husband. The only parts of me they accepted were the parts that were useful or made these men look good. I was accepted provided that I threw away any visible signs of the past me. I was accepted as long as I did what I was told.

• • •

I betrayed myself piece by piece to find some space in an overcrowded ménage à trois. Two men and a church. I had not been invited to participate, I had been invited along for the ride and only part of me could come. I would feel that truth my whole marriage long.

california.

THE MORNING AFTER our wedding, Josh and I flew to San Francisco to start our honeymoon. By the second day I had a horrible cold. In the six months since my engagement, I'd lost seven or eight pounds from all the stress of trying to please too many people, and I was run down and exhausted. I stayed in bed for three days while Josh trekked back and forth bringing me bowls of chicken noodle soup from a Jewish deli we'd found in a nearby neighborhood.

We managed to cure his virginity, but since I wasn't well, I turned him down several times on the trip. I told myself that this was only because I was sick, but in reality I wasn't as interested as I thought I would be. However, there was simply no way I was going to admit this on my honeymoon. How could a brand-new wife even entertain a thought like that? I'd just vowed to spend my life with this man. Now that we were married, it was too late to evaluate it.

• • •

We drove farther south every few days down the California coast. One night in Cambria Josh came down with a bad migraine—a foreshadowing of things to come. While he was sleeping it off in a dark room I got restless passing the time reading, so I decided to take a walk around the grounds. When I saw movement from an open door in an adjacent building I peeked my head in. A handsome, sturdy man looked up at me, smiled, and said hello. He was wearing washed blue jeans and a flannel shirt with the sleeves rolled up just so. I watched him as he shaved off long strips of wood for a piece of furniture he was building. I couldn't remember the last time I had seen a man so attractive, and I stood in the doorway a few seconds looking at him. I surprised myself when the first thought that came into my head was, *Now there's a guy I'd like to have sex with*, which was quickly followed by, *Oh my god, did I just think that on my honeymoon?* I thought about it, worried about what it could mean. Then I jiggled my head to shake the thought and went back inside to read my book.

Part Three

THE GOOD WOMAN

the joy of cooking.

BACK FROM OUR honeymoon and into our sunny, new-to-us townhouse, a huge pile of unopened wedding gifts was piled high in the corner of our unfurnished living room. I picked up the shiny new copy of the *Joy of Cooking*, one of my favorite gifts. I loved the feel of the glossy white cover and the bright red lettering. I'd decided already that I would plant my wifely stake in the ground with cooking. That would be my claim to homemaking fame, by golly.

Many of the pastors' wives had some kind of homemaking specialty or other signature talent. We were a bright and varied bunch. One woman was the Martha Stewart of the group. She sewed all her own curtains and pillows, and could whip up dinner for thirty without a lick of fluster, with six homeschooled children running underfoot. One woman made blueberry tarts and knitted adorable striped baby hats for all of our babies. She was a former NICU nurse. One woman was the humorist, always keeping it real with some brutal truth about the reality of our lives. One was a Dartmouth graduate.

One of my favorites was Julie P. She and I got to know each other when we worked at the church office together the year she moved up from Georgia. A real Southern lady, Julie was always ready with some morsel of feminine wisdom on the tip of her tongue—how to choose the right shade of lipstick, distinguishing crystal from glass, tips on seducing a husband. She was different than most of the other pastors' wives. She was confident and, because she was newer, far less affected by the church.

Our pastors' wives meetings and women's ministry sometimes made use of the different skills held by the women in our group. We covered topics like *large-group hospitality*, *meal planning*, *romancing your man*, *disciplining children*. *Contentment* was often on rotation.

But above all else there was Titus 2. Always Titus 2. That was the pinpoint, the purpose. The pinnacle of a woman's life.

> *To love their husbands and children, to be self-controlled and pure, to be busy at home, to be kind, and to be subject to their husbands, so that no one will malign the word of God.*

So I decided to master the fine art of cooking and entertaining. Because out of all the great homemaking skills one could spend their entire life learning such as gardening, laundry, dusting, and so on, it was cooking that sounded the most interesting to me. And, as I'd been combing through the chapters in the *Joy of Cooking* ever since our arrival home from the honeymoon, I was ready to begin lessons. Like any good American I went straight for the section on macaroni and cheese. There were two recipes from which to choose. One was baked and said, *A good rendition of a timeless classic.* The other was stovetop and said, *Very creamy and cheesy.* I wanted very creamy and cheesy, and I must have mentioned what I was making in passing to Josh, who naïvely suggested I get his mother's recipe. I scowled at him. I didn't want to make his mother's recipe. I wanted to make my recipe.

He continued to press. His mother's recipe was really good. It had a cheese sauce. It was baked and crispy on the top. He could call to get it. I scowled at him some more. He didn't understand what was happening here. I didn't want crispy, I wanted creamy and cheesy, and most importantly, I wanted to be in charge.

For the record it turns out his mother's recipe is better, but that was beside the point at that moment. Right then, I needed something I could own. Some space in my life that was mine. The church said it was the home. The home was *my domain.* Wouldn't that make me queen of the kitchen? But here we were arguing over mac and cheese. Was there any place where I could make the calls? I couldn't seem to find my space.

The church asked the pastors' wives to model the kind of marriages where the woman quietly recedes into the background while creating a little home haven that revolves around her husband. We were handed books with detailed specifications: Elisabeth Elliot, Martha Peace, and others. I was surrounded by Josh's mother, Sono, Carolyn, and all the women on the team—women who believed in this ideal and believed in passing it on to the next generation. I was ten or fifteen years younger than the other women on the team and new to all of this. I *was* the next generation.

That first year of marriage I was like a ball of cookie dough placed in the center of a mold and baked in the oven. When the heat hit me, I just slowly melted down into the desired shape. When I hit the walls, I accepted I could go no further. I pressed down my dreams, wants, and needs in big and small ways. I put myself under my husband—I *deferred* to him. Instead of wanting things, I was *content.* Instead of doing things I wanted to do, I *died to self.* Instead of standing up for my preferences, I just tried not to have them.

bob.

I ALSO STAYED for Bob, the music leader. I know this because years later, when our church splits into a million pieces, Bob leaves and when he does I won't want to be at church anymore. That is when I realize I stayed for him and the music.

Yes, he and I had a rocky start after my first disappointing recording session, but quickly I felt our relationship changed to one of mutual respect. Early on I asked for something to do at Josh's conferences. Smiling and nodding for two hours by Josh's side turned into me having a spot to perform a song. Bob accompanied me on the piano, and together we had a certain synergy. I sang a song I loved at the time called "Who Am I," written by Christy and Nathan Nockels.

After this, Bob began to include me in just about all his musical projects. Or at least it seemed that way. I am sure there were many things I wasn't getting to do as a woman, such as training, leadership, composing, or writing songs. But back then I wasn't questioning it or thinking about the things I wasn't doing. I was constantly working on something. Either rehearsing for a Sunday service, preparing a solo for holiday, recording in the studio, or traveling across the country to sing at a conference or a festival.

Music was one place in the church I felt I held my own. I played with the big boys. I was in their space, I was on their flights. It felt really good and really right for me to be there. I was just as comfortable and confident in the recording room as I was singing in front of five thousand people. I was happy on the stage, and singing with Bob accompanying me always felt magical.

the maternity dress.

BEFORE THE END of the first year of marriage, I was pregnant. I spent the first five and a half months with hyperemesis gravidarum (head over the toilet) and the rest of the time trying to find relief from bulging varicose veins. I was wearing black medical tights that made me hot and sweaty and even more miserable. So just to recap, I was a slow-moving, starving, vomiting, bulging, sweating woman.

Finally, the nausea lessened just enough for me to manage singing for the Sunday service. I had recently purchased a sweet new maternity dress, which I wore to sing in that Sunday. It was heather gray and simple, and I had on the black medical tights and a clunky pair of black shoes. There was nothing remotely sexy or even fashionable about this outfit, I assure you.

Yet at my next mentoring coffee time with Carolyn, just after the small talk there was an uncomfortable silence. By this time I'd experienced enough of these moments to know I was about to be confronted. I couldn't wait to hear what I'd done wrong this time.

"Do you think your dress was immodest on Sunday?" she asked. Then as usual, the awkward pause.

My first thought was to wonder if that was a trick question and if grammar had anything to do with it. I felt my heart start to pound hard against my chest while I wracked my brain trying to recall what I had worn. I quickly sorted the data: a protruding belly, a tall stage, and an accidentally shrunken dress made of Lycra. From Carolyn's front row vantage point she (or someone) must have been looking straight up my dress.

It was an honest oversight on my part. But clearly someone thought I was trying to show off a little of my sexy medical tights. Or hoping the congregation would start stuffing dollar bills in the tights. Anyway, I never wore the dress again. But it was moments like this that reminded me of the uncomfortable reality that I lived with, which was that I was always being watched and monitored. If I wore a dress that was three inches too short, someone noticed. If I said something wrong, someone noticed. If I got too close to people, someone noticed.

I received the heaviest amounts of confrontation in my formative years there, first when I joined the music team and then again when I came under the church's thumb as Josh's wife, and this shaped me for the rest of my years at church. I also watched how CJ managed the other pastors and wives. I was taking notes. He created a culture where criticism, evaluation, and even humiliation were normalized and reframed as love. I shrunk back to protect myself. I did not want confrontations and meetings being held about me. I did not want to make a mistake and get my husband fired. I was outgoing and friendly, but I stopped sharing my deeper self. I conformed myself to fit into the quietest, smallest shell possible. And the shell came to feel almost normal. But not really. I was always working at staying small.

spankings.

I WAS AN anxious mother, which will come as no surprise. Though apart from the church I don't think I would have been. But as it was, as pastors' families, it was expected that our kids be well behaved. It was made clear to me that if my children did not grow up to meet the church's standards my husband could be disqualified from ministry. So when my first baby came, my anxiety went through the roof and never left. Feeling that your kids *have* to turn out a certain way is no way to be a mother. And *having* to turn out a certain way is no way to be a kid.

• • •

When Emma was about two years old she and I were going to the home of another pastor's wife so Emma could play with her little girl. Esther and Joe were a new addition to our pastoral team, a young Korean American couple. I was so happy when Esther came on because she was my age and because Esther was different. She wasn't going to play the good woman game. Esther said out loud all the things I was thinking in my head. She was so real in the pastors' wives meetings that whenever she'd share her personal struggles everyone would stare and blink afterward. That's because they'd just been hit with more truth bombs in ten minutes than they'd heard all month. I always found it extremely entertaining.

When my daughter and I got to Esther's she was in the kitchen boiling some beef and saying she had to boil all the blood out of it. I wasn't sure how that could possibly taste good, but what did I know about Korean cooking? Everything I'd ever eaten of Esther's was delicious. There was an enormous kimchi refrigerator in the corner of her kitchen. I couldn't understand how someone could need an appliance this big just for kimchi. And beef. Esther was constantly expanding my way of thinking.

We put the girls in the basement where all the toys were and Esther poured me a cup of coffee. Maybe we'd get thirty minutes to talk before someone started screaming. Esther was frustrated that day because spanking wasn't really working on her daughter and she could only take her into the bathroom so many times before it started to feel cruel. Spankings usually happened in the bathroom. I guess it was supposed to make it less humiliating for your child while you were pulling down their pants.

I usually used a wooden spoon or this rubber paddle someone had given us called a *wisdom wacker.* I liked it because it was flexible and seemed less traumatic to administer, especially for the one administering. I found out later that my kids preferred the wooden spoon. Either way, I hated spanking, and I would not do it if I were to have children all over again. The deal was, you were not supposed to do it angry, but even for me it could feel like a muddled line sometimes. When your kid is screaming in your ear at 120 decibels your blood is practically curdling inside you. You're only human.

That muddled line is what makes children and discipline a dangerous business. When does "faithful discipline" turn into abuse? How would a child know the difference between a proper expectation of obedience and an improper one? Spare the rod, spoil the child might have been OK for the seventeenth century, but we know way too much now.

I was lucky to have it easy with Emma. She was that kid who fools you into believing you know what you are doing as a parent. She could look at books for two hours on her bed. She stood beside me nicely at church. She let me be her authority, so I didn't have to work too hard at it. Still, I hated spanking her. My second child would be much less interested in following said program. My third child would agree with the second.

But there we were—two young moms, sipping our coffee, feeling the pressure to satisfy all the expectations required of us—our children, our husbands, the rules of the church. We both sat silently mulling this over when one of the kids started to scream.

migraines.

WE WERE SITTING in the kitchen eating beef stew for dinner one evening when suddenly Josh said he felt sick. He got up from the table to go upstairs and the next thing I knew I heard him vomiting. I thought it was my cooking. He didn't reemerge until the next day.

The migraines started the first year we were married. They often came on Mondays, Josh's only day off each week. Perhaps it was the excitement, stress, and subsequent letdown of preaching on Sundays. I'd start the day out hopeful to have some adult conversation or help with the kids, and by late morning he might have a headache and need to lie down in our darkened, quiet bedroom.

We tried hard to determine the cause. His headaches seemed to be food related, so we began to eliminate foods that bothered him. First, he thought it was the garlic. I'd stop cooking with garlic and then onion would bother him, so I'd stop cooking with onion. Then it was ascorbic acid, which is in almost every can of tomatoes in the universe. Then jam would seem to bother him, so I'd cut out anything with pectin. Then it was MSG, and chili powder, and then yeast extract and carrageenan, and meats that were cooked too long or injected with solution.

I bought an enormous stockpot and boiled chickens to freeze homemade broth for flavoring dishes, until that stopped working too. I shopped at multiple grocery and specialty stores. I cooked and packed him three days' worth of food whenever he traveled. Everything took longer—the planning, the shopping, the cooking. I couldn't just pick up a rotisserie chicken or order a pizza. For years both the menu and Josh got thinner.

kind of deceptive.

WE'D ONLY BEEN at the townhouse on Fountain Valley a few short years. I was happy there. Very happy, actually. I adored the house and had just finished painting the dining room, recovering chairs, and hanging a pair of floral tab top curtains that I made, all the while hugely pregnant with my second child. I was just starting to make the house a home, and I was thrilled because some other couples our age had been added to our team, and two of those couples had purchased homes in the same neighborhood, including Esther. I was starting to envision our kids growing up in the neighborhood together.

But just at that time CJ suggested to Josh that now was a good time for us to move into a single-family home. The reason he gave was that it would be better for us to purchase a nicer house before the *transition* took place than after. (The transition was when CJ would hand off the leadership of the church to Josh.) The assumption was that everyone would be watching more closely and we wouldn't want to appear too extravagant. I couldn't make up my mind if that was *kind* or *kind of deceptive* for a pastor.

But when CJ said jump we were very much still jumping. So just after I had my second child, we bought the house on Plum Creek. It was a 1970s brick colonial sitting on two acres in a beautiful neighborhood that had once been an orchard. It needed remodeling, but I fell for the long driveway and wide streets and three magnificent oak trees in the backyard—all things that I wanted for my children.

Sometimes I wonder if I chose the Plum Creek house because it felt protected and safe at a time when it was not safe to be me. It was set far back from the road and partially hidden by enormous old pines. I could raise my children there and let them run in the wide, open yard and they would be safe. Maybe at least they could feel free.

tentacles.

IF THE REQUIREMENTS for women's roles had simply stuck to the originals (helper, working in the home, raising children) the whole biblical submission thing might have stayed believable. But the requirements grew like the tentacles of an octopus searching for food in the crevices of our lives. Had we all attained the basic submissive womanhood sufficiently enough that now we were moving up to an advanced version? Or were they just keeping us occupied like babies in a playpen? The bar kept moving, raising, evolving, and before long, it began to venture into the absurd. Like the time the pastors' wives got in trouble for studying theology on a Saturday while drinking up sunshine and coffee.

That particular morning, I ran out early to get some bagels. As I was walking up to the shop I saw about five of our pastors' wives under an umbrella having a casual study time outside. They were using Wayne Grudem's *Systematic Theology*, a massive book and required reading for any male Pastor's College student in our denomination. Julie, the Southern one, was leading the study. Incidentally, Julie's husband happened to be the only executive with a degree in theology, and he was the dean of our Pastor's College. Regardless, she was more than capable.

After greeting the women, I went in to buy my bagels. Back at home I casually mentioned to Josh that I'd seen the women studying and was feeling a little sad I hadn't been invited, but that I thought it was great they were doing it. I never gave it a second thought. But a few days later I heard a meeting had been called and it was to be held in our home. This had never happened before, so it was suspect to me. Why was this meeting called in our home?

At the meeting I discovered that either CJ or Carolyn (or both) wanted to shut the group down. We were already the only church in the area that didn't have women's Bible studies. Now they had a problem with women studying theology in their own free time? Our theology restricted women from teaching the Bible to men. But now they were taking this theology and stretching it further. I thought this was ridiculous. The thought of restricting anyone's learning about anything really hit a nerve with me and though I said nothing, I could see that I was not on the same page with Carolyn and CJ anymore, and my collection of reasons was slowly growing.

you have to like it.

JOSH AND I usually argued about one of three things: food, decorating, and minivans. Given that we had just purchased a new house, this fight was about decorating. Or rather Josh hoping to convince me *not* to decorate because it always caused him a lot of stress thanks to the fact that I am woefully indecisive.

I can trace my indecisiveness back to how my parents handled their divorce. Both my parents are wonderful and supportive and loving. They even like each other as friends. And as they say, "If they had known better, they would have done better." But they made one small mistake in raising me that I have forgiven them for, but can't fix. When my parents divorced they followed the bad counsel of an Episcopal priest, a family friend, who suggested my brother and I be given the chance to choose which parent we wanted to live with. I was ten years old at that time. My brother spoke up first, choosing Dad. That left me in the awful position of having to choose between my parents. I didn't want my mom, who was needing to move for a job, to be all alone, but I also didn't want to lose my sibling or my friends. And the thing about emotional distress is that once you've had it, it can reappear to torment you at any moment, even if you are just scrambling eggs.

So what this means for me is that whenever I make a decision about anything, even paint colors—let's say I have to decide between Benjamin Moore Owl Gray and Classic Gray. One of them is the right choice and leads to everlasting joy, and one of them is the wrong choice and leads to suffering and death, and I am not sure which is which. And whatever poor soul cohabitates with me has to watch me agonize over this at length. Josh had gotten frustrated with me and was trying to shut down the project altogether, and I was trying to push it forward when everything came to a head.

I stormed out of the house angry and slammed the door. Suddenly I was standing outside on a dark, chilly night and kicking myself for not bringing a jacket, so I could stay out longer to prove how angry I was. I didn't last long out there and when I returned, Josh informed me that he'd called CJ and Carolyn and they were coming over to help us with the argument. They came, listened, talked about their own disagreements and ways to reconnect. I thought we'd gotten it sorted out. But no. The next day I was down in the basement attempting to homeschool two children and entertain a toddler when Carolyn called to follow up. The point of her call was to ask how much sex I was initiating. This, the church's solution for all types of marital discord.

"I'm not initiating," I said. "I don't like it." A rare moment of brutal honesty.

Without skipping a beat she answered, "Well, you *have* to like it."

nipples and all.

I DON'T KNOW about you, but I dress for success. And during my church days, success meant never again being reprimanded for my body parts or clothing. I'm not sure if it was the maternity dress that pushed me over the edge or the time my nipples came up for discussion at the church office. Hard to say.

So before going to church or meetings or even the grocery, I carefully constructed my outfits to make sure they fit the part. I'd check to make sure that my blouse wasn't gaping and that my jeans weren't too tight. I checked the mirror multiple times before I walked out the door. Multiple times.

Not drawing attention to yourself. It was a phrase I heard often and man if it wasn't a mood killer. It's hard to be alive and not draw attention to yourself. When a person speaks they are drawing attention to themselves. When someone shares an opinion or laughs they are drawing attention to themselves. When a person wears bright colors or lipstick they are drawing attention to themselves.

Modesty is one of those catch-all words that the church loves. It becomes a sort of broom and is used to shoo away all kinds of unwanted behavior according to personal preference. I used to think of clothing mostly when I heard the word *modesty*, but I realize now it is more all-encompassing than that. Modesty is a state of being. What the church was really asking was for women to diminish themselves in any and every way. This one tiny, soft-sounding word was actually razor sharp. In one fell swoop it cut us down to smaller size saying, *Be less. Less visible. Less loud. Less colorful. Less present.*

The word was also used to manage the "problem" of female sexuality, only this time it said, *Be less sexual.* It put the onus on women to provide the answer for male temptation. By being less attractive, by changing our dress or behavior or by being sexually available the message was clear: women were responsible or could be held responsible for the way men behave. In reality, each of us is responsible for our own actions.

• • •

So no matter what someone says, don't become less to make someone else more comfortable. You don't need to hide your talents or opinions or your beauty or even your sexuality. Don't offer less of your presence, offer more. If someone has a problem with that, let them deal with it, not you. You belong here, nipples and all.

baton passing.

IN 2004 THE *transition* came. By now the church had grown to be over three thousand members and we had about twenty-five pastors. We were in a new, enormous sanctuary and outgrowing even that. CJ had been prepping everyone for this moment for years, which I suspect was actually a sales pitch, since Joshua's notoriety attracted many new, young families to the church. A celebratory event was held. My husband assumed leadership of the church while CJ was to turn his attention to leading the parent ministry, Sovereign Grace Ministries. To most people watching, the transition probably appeared seamless.

It had not occurred to me that CJ and Carolyn might stay close after the transition. I mean, I assumed they'd be around, but I'd always heard that CEOs leave the premises when they hand the company over to someone new. I thought they were supposed to go to Tahiti, rent a yacht for a while, and then start consulting work. I thought we would be given some space. I thought it was good of CJ to be willing to give my husband a chance to lead while he was young. But when the transition happened very little actually changed. CJ moved only one chair over. At meetings he sat right next to Josh whispering in his ear.

I became the new senior pastor's wife, but in name only. Carolyn maintained her position as leader of women's ministry. If it had been any other church in our ministry, this role would have fallen to me. But this was still very much CJ and Carolyn's church. It never came up how I would contribute now that my role had changed. Carolyn brought her daughters on to lead the women's ministry with her, which meant I had been right all those years ago; there was no place they envisioned for me in the church. Fortunately, there was no role I wanted in this show.

feminine wounds.

SOMETIME AFTER THE transition apparently someone had an idea of how my role could change. It turned out my role was expanding after all. I was being promoted from victim to perpetrator.

I was given a small group of women to lead in my new role. And the first task given to me by Carolyn was to tell a new pastor's wife joining our group that her new position meant she could not pursue her dream career in veterinary medicine. What? Did I hear that correctly? Me? A new young couple had just joined our team and delivering the death of a dream was now my job? I'll never forget Carolyn's voice the day she told me I was to do this. She must have been relieved to pass this task off to me. My heart sank. It felt like a bait and switch. I did not want to tell another woman that she couldn't have her dreams.

It was a Sunday afternoon. My group of five women and I filed into a local café and sat down. To my eyes, everyone appeared to be moving in slow motion. My insides were wretched like the day at the ocean. I couldn't eat. I couldn't drink. I remember nothing about the meeting except the task I had to fulfill. It was like a scene in a movie where the lead character is on a boat and needing to carry out a murder before the end of the night is up. I had to use the meeting to hunt and kill someone's dream.

I remember the blur, I remember my anxiousness, and I remember saying the words. I remember nothing else about the meeting except the look on this brilliant woman's face after I told her, and the silence of everyone afterward. But I did it. This time I was the cruel one, forcing obedience and conformity on a person I was supposed to love and care for.

This event changed me. After that day I determined that I would never police other women in this way if I could help it. It was at this juncture that I separated myself from Carolyn in my mind and heart. Maybe this was her idea of a pastor's wife, but it was not mine. I would do this my own way.

his wife.

CELEBRITY LIFE DOES have its perks. My husband was now an international best-selling author and in-demand as a speaker and evangelical leader. Sometimes we traveled together as a team when he spoke. We were always well cared for by our hosts. The gift baskets were lovely. The pay was generous.

People thought we were wonderful, although they thought it for all the wrong reasons. They believed we were somehow more holy than they were. Or that we had found the key to marital bliss. Or that we were wise beyond our years. We were none of those things.

But my point here is how I was treated at these speaking engagements by leaders. This was a man's world, and as a woman in it, I was often overlooked. It wasn't at all unusual for me to be introduced to the people in those settings as *his wife* or not be introduced at all. Eventually, I made a game out of it to see how long it took men to acknowledge me. They got points for eye contact, more points for a handshake, and even more points if they said my name. The winner of my game was the man who invited me into a conversation with genuine interest. (There weren't many.) I'm sure people meant no disrespect for me. They were there to hear Josh speak, but I had way more to offer than a smile.

To be clear, most of the male leaders in my own church treated me with dignity and respect. We got to know each other quite well through the years with the many meetings and discussions we had, frequently in my home. I had my favorites with whom I was able to connect and share ideas. Still, the culture of our church meant that the men held priority in whatever space we were in. Wives were viewed as inferior and adjunct. Men did most of the talking, women did most of the smiling and nodding.

This behavior spilled over into my married life with Josh. I went along quietly listening, not sharing my opinions, expecting him to do the thinking for both of us. It was a role I played well, but it never felt natural. I wanted to support my husband. I used my personal power in making a lovely home, teaching my children, providing healthy meals, and caring for the people in my church.

Being his wife also meant that we were always "on." Even our private life was subservient to my husband's career and the church. One Valentine's dinner I wanted to have a glass of wine and Josh asked me not to for fear it would get back to someone higher up. One day I came home to discover my childhood music collection had been thrown away for the very same reason. I had to return the prenatal yoga video I purchased in case someone saw it and thought we were turning Buddhist. Big church brother was watching over us all the time. This became very draining for me. There was no place, public or private, where I could let my hair down and relax.

five o'clock club.

HONESTLY, I WAS an unlikely candidate for a pastor's wife from the start. I didn't grow up with the Bible. I have to stop and remember whether Cain or Abel is the vegetarian. I get mixed up with those two guys—Elisha and Elijah. And if I'm being totally honest, I find Bible reading laborious—especially if I'm being made to do it. Back at church people were encouraged to read their Bible for an hour daily. In churches all over the world this is called a quiet time and it's the badge of the good Christian. I knew some people who actually did this for a whole hour and loved it. Personally, I think those people were either truly beautiful souls, scholars, or lying. I usually cheated and read the *Joy of Cooking* for a good bit of it. Thanks to quiet times, I am now a very good cook.

But I think it was when Carolyn launched her Five O'Clock Club that I'd finally had enough. She was suggesting women get up at five o'clock in the morning to do their quiet time. I may have believed in God, but I also believed in sleep. Weren't we already doing enough between our husbands and kids and homeschooling and volunteering and throwing baby showers and all the rest that life brings? I hadn't managed to be all that successful with seven o'clock, so if they wanted me to wake up at five they were going to have to do more than just invite me to a club. They would need to start paying me or injecting me with some really good amphetamines.

homesteading.

I'VE COME TO believe that if a woman isn't given any place to grow outside of her home she has no choice but to try and grow inside it. But at some point we will have made everything there is to make and learned all there is to learn and we'll be reaching further and further just to keep on growing. That, my friends, is how a woman ends up fermenting sauerkraut when she is supposed to be working at whatever it is that makes her truly happy.

I can't claim that I was ever a truly excellent homemaker, but I was especially good at pretending to be one. I was very good at owning a wonderful assortment of expensive kitchen appliances I hardly ever used. I had a juicer, a grain mill, a five-pound German pickling crock, an industrial-sized mixer, and a second refrigerator-freezer in the garage. Having all of these tools was handy in making the act more believable for myself.

I kept myself busy by creating new homemaking jobs for myself. I learned to cook anything and everything from scratch. I learned to host dinners and parties. I took up sewing and quilting. I read Emily Post's *Etiquette* and Cheryl Mendelson's *Home Comforts* in my free time.

And though I never made my own mint pies, I did try freezer cooking, but it never was my style. My journal says that one afternoon I made six pounds of sloppy joe mix, two batches of homemade cream of mushroom soup, twelve marinated buttermilk herb chicken breasts, two 9x11 pans of a Hallelujah Halibut, and pulled the meat off seven roasted chickens.

When my kids got to school age, I threw myself into homeschooling. It was the first time I had complete and total autonomy. No one cared what I did and no one hovered. I approached this in the same way that I approached most of the things I had done in life—full on. Studying, learning, trying, and practicing until I'd mastered it to the degree that I wanted.

I learned to be a good teacher. A good teacher is a performer, which tapped right into who I was. I built a huge library. I taught each of my children to read and write. We spent afternoons in nature drawing pictures of insects and flowers. Together we learned art, music, literature, and history. I tried to nurture their interests and give them a glimpse of how much there was in the world to learn.

The years at the Plum Creek house were the best time in our family life. I hunkered down there and nested. I was so happy that I could stay home with my children for their young years. It was a luxury. And in many ways I was the mother I had always wanted to be.

But I never stopped having the desire to fulfill my own dreams or the feeling that I was supposed to. My dream was always with me. I just couldn't attend to it at that time. I held it in a special place I now call *things that mattered to me.*

Eventually I grew tired. Our intense schedule meant there was little time for rest. I was wife, mother, pastor's wife, teacher, cook, housekeeper, babymaker, and kitchen help.

I felt alone in most of these roles and I found myself longing for time to be creative and to do work I chose for myself. The pep talks in my mind began to occur with more frequency. *You love this work, Shannon. You love this work. You are helping your husband, you are helping your husband.* Still, my love of music and my dream sat in my belly like an unwatered seed calling, *Don't forget me, don't forget me.*

The enormous capacity of women to enlarge resources is one of the reasons I think we stay too long in places where we are no longer thriving. We are good at stretching the goodness. But sometimes you have done all you can do. You have outgrown the pot and though you keep reaching, you know you are not thriving. The only thing to do then is die or find a bigger piece of earth.

Part Four

UNDOINGS

(Six Years Later)

a bit of earth.

I WAS DRIVING all over Timbuktu to get raw milk and meat not injected with hormones. And to see a creepy dentist who wanted to take out all my mercury fillings. Along with all of that nonsense I must have decided that it was a good time to start growing my own vegetables and living off the land. But I didn't take time to plan my garden like a normal person would have. Instead, I grabbed the shovel one day on a whim and dug up a large 8x8 patch of grass in the backyard.

It was way more work than I thought it was going to be, because the ground was hard and I couldn't get down very deep. Even so I dug enough to have an enormous pile of grass and dirt that needed to be dealt with afterward, which I also hadn't foreseen. I stuck the shovel in the ground and went back inside, regretting that I had attempted the garden at all.

Days went by and I didn't plant anything on account of the family of deer that walked through our yard every day. They would surely devour everything in sight if I didn't put up a fence. I casually suggested to my husband that maybe we could hire someone to build a fence. He didn't seem too keen on that, so I googled *how to build a garden fence* and watched a few videos. I decided that it was above my skill level and my pay grade, so the project stalled.

For the next few weeks every time I looked out the kitchen window my eye went directly to the patch of ground that I'd dug up in my otherwise picturesque backyard. There was something unrelenting about it. I washed the dishes and looked at the stupid patch. Washed the dishes and looked at the stupid patch.

One day I was washing the dishes and looking at the stupid patch and I had the moment of epiphany that had been quietly brewing for years. *What the hell am I doing right now? I don't even like gardening. What the hell am I doing with any of this? What the hell am I doing with my whole life?*

My life had no meaning, no depth beyond the church. I was restricted to the real and imaginary walls of the church. I was nothing outside its purview. Sunday to Sunday, every day of the week, I was held hostage by my role in this church. I had swallowed the grape juice and it had swallowed me. My husband didn't take me out dancing. I didn't have friends outside of the church. Everything outside the church was viewed as evil.

After that, I never went back to the garden. The garden of Eden, that is.

death.

IN SPRING OF 2010, Josh and I flew out to Oregon to see his sister Sarah in a play. The night we got there Josh's mother, while eating a bowl of homemade quark, told us that she had been diagnosed with incurable, stage 4 cancer. The announcement sent my mind reeling. She was too young to die. How devastating this would be for Josh and all the kids. Only four out of seven of her children were fully grown. How would their father manage alone? I wondered anxiously if I might be needed to help raise these children in addition to my own.

A several-weeks-long family gathering on the Harris property was organized so we could spend time together before she died. Our family piled into a room above the garage, and we slept on spare cushions and air mattresses. Our kids were ten, eight, and four. Two of the kids came down with fevers. I started running on autopilot. I did more cooking and cleaning up than I had the energy for. When I should have been resting I spent the afternoons butchering a freezer full of whole, organic chickens that Josh's mother had ordered. I didn't want them to go to waste, as if that mattered. And while I was butchering chickens all I could think about was how in the world I was going to keep my kids from falling behind in math. This was the summer we were going to catch up. His mom died a few weeks later.

• • •

Six months later my brother's wife, who was already sick and waiting for a liver transplant, fell backward going down the stairs and hit her head, sending her into a coma. She was placed on life support and died about a month later. She left a six-year-old behind. Our family was suddenly filled with motherless children.

The contrast between these two situations didn't fully register in my mind then, but I certainly felt it. We had dropped everything and moved to Oregon for three weeks while Josh's mother was sick. But when my family was in crisis it was business as usual. Our schedule kept on churning, and I struggled to find time to offer support for my brother, who lived just an hour away.

It's obvious now that all I had to do was speak up. State my needs. Say that I wanted to spend time with my brother, his wife, and their young son. I loved them. They were my family. But why couldn't I see or do that? My personal power wasn't available to me any longer. It had been tucked away and hidden somewhere long ago when I joined the church. I had lost the key. Buried it. Forgotten about it. I wouldn't have even known to search for it. But I was starting to miss it.

the documents.

July 2011

WE WERE ON vacation in Sarasota, Florida, when Josh got a phone call. I heard his voice sink two octaves. Recent months had been tenuous ones for the denomination. For more than five years, some of CJ's key leaders had been trying to address patterns they'd seen in his leadership such as hypocrisy and deceit, but had yet to reach a satisfying resolution. The constant tension surrounding CJ had been building and had now come to a head. Listening to Josh take stressful phone calls like this had become a regular part of my life.

When the call ended, Josh told me that one of CJ's founding partners had compiled a third collection of documents—hundreds of pages of emails, letters, meeting notes, and other not-so-shiny personal information intended to show evidence for the concerns the men had been trying to raise with CJ. This time the pages included evidence of blackmail. What's more, someone had leaked the pages onto the internet. Soon the whole ministry would be aware there was trouble in the kingdom.

Here was CJ's opportunity to show us all that he was capable of taking what he dished out. This time he was the one in the hot seat and the entire ministry was watching. Unfortunately, he didn't take it. Not in my opinion. At our annual Leaders Conference I found the words he shared to be remarkably brief and avoidant and caused people to have to choose sides. Then, CJ simply walked off the stage and out of our lives. He abruptly severed ties with Josh and me and any others who could not, or would not, absolve him of all responsibility. He announced he was moving the ministry headquarters to another state and began packing immediately. Divisions everywhere followed—within our team, within our church, within the denomination. Even family members were split apart. I never again heard from Bob, Carolyn, or the handful of other pastors and wives who went with CJ.

Initially, I was blindsided by CJ's response. I still wanted to believe the best about CJ. But his reaction changed my view once and for all. I thought, "My God, we really are in Oz." There were many things that were still unclear to me, but one thing was clear. In the hour when people most needed a shepherd and a leader, when the past came to be reckoned with, when the house the man built was burning, his choice was to leave it behind and start over someplace else. *The greatest place on Earth?* Eh, they can save themselves.

tulips.

CJ WAS PACKING up the headquarters of the ministry and moving to Kentucky with some of our team. I debated at length about whether or not I should say goodbye in person to three of the women who were special to me. Each of their husbands was aligning with CJ, and everyone on their side of the situation had gone radio silent.

It seemed wrong to me to not say goodbye. Julie P. had been a very close friend. Nancy had been a true mentor to me. And Julie K., Bob's wife, had been an important figure in my life. I decided I would regret it one day if I didn't at least try to make peace. I made up three glass mason jars with a bunch of yellow tulips and tied a ribbon around each one. Yellow for friendship.

I couldn't believe that after fifteen years of shared life—ladies' meetings, getaway retreats, high teas, pizzas, bridal showers, weddings, women's events, babies, conferences with our husbands, conferences without our husbands, picnics, homeschooling, tears, celebrations, prayers, Starbucks, screaming toddlers, meals for births and illnesses, apple picking, pumpkin patches, Christmas parties, meetings, meetings, and more meetings—our relationships were ending like this.

I wondered how I would be received when I showed up. Maybe when I got there we would hug or smile weak but knowing smiles in a brief ceremonial moment as if to say, *This era of our life is over.* I understood they had no choice but to support their husbands—and I was hoping they'd understand I didn't either. Wasn't this literally what Carolyn had been teaching us all to do for the past fifteen years? Support our men? So what if our men had fallen on different sides of the equation. We could still have sisterhood.

I went to Julie P.'s house first. It felt strange to be so nervous to visit someone who once was one of my dearest friends. She was cold, and her eyes told me I was dead to her. I gave her the flowers, a hug, and told her I loved her, and then I left. Julie K. was next. Same scene. Cold eyes, I gave her the flowers, I told her I loved her, and I left. At Nancy's, no one answered the door. I left her tulips on the porch and said goodbye to the air.

• • •

The church split and all that came with it devastated me. My whole world just crumbled in an instant. Relationships I'd built my life around just turned to dust in my hands. CJ and Carolyn were not the people I thought they were. The abrupt loss of friendships felt like multiple deaths at once. And the hypocrisy of it all was too much to take. To have heard the words *forgiveness* and *grace* in hundreds of sermons, thousands of prayers, in every quote, every song, at every meeting and then to discover that in real life it had no impact on our actual relationships . . . I had never experienced something so deeply and profoundly disturbing in all my life.

despair.

I STILL HAD to go back and be the pastor's wife for my grieving church. I saw firsthand the wreckage left behind when a leader refuses to face his own humanity. Our congregation was hurting, confused, angry, disillusioned, and they had every right to be. In public I appeared strong. But at home I was drowning in grief of my own. We watched a lot of people leave the church that year.

Just when I was beginning to accept the events of the past year an even more serious crisis emerged when allegations of a sexual abuse cover-up were brought to the church. Multiple instances of abuse had occurred during the 1980s at the hands of a duplicitous, unofficial church leader who had gained the trust of the pastors and had open access to children. The situation had apparently been handled in-house while CJ was the senior pastor. Now the victims were seeking justice.

A whirlwind followed, complete with national news coverage, and Josh, as the current head pastor, was at the center of it all. To me, he appeared to be being attacked from all sides while scrambling to piece together what had happened. Later I would wonder if CJ had intentionally put my husband in leadership knowing that this storm was brewing. Had he purposely gotten himself out of the spotlight? Though my husband eventually realized that he too had been culpable, it was hard not to feel that CJ abandoned him to take the fall for a disaster that occurred under his leadership.

Meanwhile Josh's nineteen-year-old sister Sarah came to live with us. We had a basement apartment that was almost always rented out. It was currently occupied, so I didn't have a proper bedroom to give her. I moved the kids' school room to the upstairs and set up a makeshift bedroom for her there.

Sarah was going through a lot, having lost her mother. Josh was navigating the sexual abuse allegations at church. And I was a walking zombie. Unbeknownst to me I had developed PTSD. I had no room for Sarah's pain, and I was too numb to even feel guilty about it. I could give her a bed and I think we helped her find a counselor and I don't even know if I cooked her food. I know she ate a lot of ramen noodles. She got a job at Chick-Fil-A and took a ridiculously long walk on top of a bus ride to get there every day. About a year later, when she got engaged, I was finally able to do something for her. She was still dealing with the trauma of losing her mother and didn't want to plan her own wedding, so I offered to do it for her.

The wedding solidified my detachment from my problems and my real life. I was not in connection with myself, I was a robot. I thought nothing. I felt nothing. I moved through checklists. The flowers, the menu, the cheese tasting. I repainted walls in the house. I pulled up all the landscaping out front and planted new plants. But my body was telling the real story. One night while getting a glass of water in the middle of the night I crumpled unconscious into a heap on the floor. Earlier, I had miscarried a child. And depression had moved in to stay.

It was here that I had my breakdown that I told you about in the very beginning of my story. When I handed the kids to my husband and locked myself in my bedroom for three days and thought about becoming Catholic and said I couldn't keep going to church. The precise dates are fuzzy. But the important details are:

Sarah got married and moved out.

I asked our renters to leave so I wouldn't have to say hello.

I canceled hosting people at our house for the year.

And I tried to disappear.

fulcrum year.

"THIS WAS SUPPOSED to be your year of creativity!" my mom exclaimed.

"I know, Mom. Soon," I said, sorting through boxes while I held the phone up to my ear. "Maybe next year."

We were moving across town trying to get a fresh start. I was culling and sorting through our belongings because the new townhouse was about half the size of our sprawling Plum Creek home. I'd tried to get out of it—the moving. The night before we signed the contract I got cold feet and begged Josh not to have us do it. I had gone down to the basement and taken one look at all of our belongings, and it hit me what we were about to do. All the boxes and the work and the energy and decision-making it was going to take, and I almost died. And I loved our home and I didn't really want to move. What I really wanted was more time for things that mattered to me. We had talked about giving me more time for things that mattered to me. But somehow it turned into moving.

We gave or sold much of our furniture away to church people in a massive weekend free-for-all. Josh sent out an email and posted it on Facebook, and the response was instantaneous. Feeling unfastened, I made myself scarce and greeted almost no one. I watched from the window as people from church drove up with their trucks and left with our belongings.

• • •

Just before we moved I cut my hair into a super-short pixie. It was disproportionately liberating. It was odd, but the haircut made me feel happier than I'd been in years. If you had seen me then, you would have thought I'd just found the courage to run off to Italy or conduct a bank heist. I got some bounce back, and I couldn't have explained why if you had asked. But the reason was that without intending to I had reclaimed a piece of me. When I cut my hair it didn't matter to me if Josh liked it. It wasn't for him or anyone else. It was something I did 100 percent for me. And every fiber of my being was applauding.

• • •

At the new townhouse, there was an unsettled vibe. It was a weird year. A pivot year. Like our lives had been on one side of a seesaw, and this year was the fulcrum. Soon we'd be tipping the other direction.

I put the kids in the church school that year for the first time, a decision so agonizing you would have thought we were leaving them to be raised by vampires. It was a relief for me, but what I really wanted for the kids was something much different. Something *not* at church. Their world was too small.

• • •

"Let's just move into the wilderness somewhere and live in a cabin," I said half seriously. "We can live off the land and go down to the river and catch fish for dinner. I don't care if we have any money." I saw a glimmer flash across Josh's face. He actually liked my idea.

I was actually kind of serious. I needed change, and I was grasping at straws. He was tired too. Which was good, because if he wanted to keep being a pastor at this church he was going to have to explain why his wife was no longer attending.

Around this time we heard about some counselors in Kentucky who specialized in helping burnt-out pastors. We heard they worked with pastors from some of the largest churches in the United States. Pastors who were suicidal and barely making it out of bed in the morning. I wasn't sure if the counselors helped the wives of these men, but either way I wanted to meet with them.

It was a big deal that we were looking to go outside the ministry for counseling. No one went outside the ministry for anything, particularly counseling. Some of the men on our team even pushed back on the idea, our world was so insular. One of the counselors had a twenty-five-year career as a pastor in addition to a PhD in counseling. It was hard to imagine finding someone being more qualified to help us.

"I don't care what anyone thinks. We are going," I said.

• • •

Rich and Jim met with us for two whole days.

I expected it to go like so many meetings in the past twenty years had. We'd show up, Josh would do most of the talking, I would smile and nod my head. Josh would speak for us, decide for us, and basically *be* us. But it went nothing like that. Here was a man, actually two men, who were listening to me, seeing me, hearing me. I was not *his wife* in this room. I was a person. I was me, *Shannon*.

I went in there thinking I was going crazy. I left sane and relieved. I wasn't crazy for wanting to leave ministry. *That* ministry. In fact, what was crazy is that we had lasted as long as we did.

At one point during the counseling Rich asked us a simple question. "What do you want?"

What do I want? The question washed over me like a forgotten waterfall in some lagoon I used to swim in. I couldn't remember the last time I had asked myself that. Or felt safe enough to even try. I said it over again in my mind. *What do I want . . . What do I want . . . What do I want?*

What I wanted was to feel happy. And I wanted not to feel like the kids and I were on display. I wanted to have a career of my own in music or theater. And I wanted my life to matter as much as my husband's did.

glass ceiling.

WE CAME BACK from the weekend of counseling and asked for a six-month sabbatical. It had been sixteen years of ministry without an extended break. Maybe some rest was all we needed. Meanwhile, Josh and I discussed what our next steps would be if our request was denied and we decided to take a break from ministry.

I was so hopeful for the future because this was the first time I, the woman in this scene, had been acknowledged as a separate person. I began to see and understand the vast double standard that *was* my marriage. These counselors had reminded me and affirmed that I could and should have my own goals and personal values. It had been over fifteen years since I had heard anything like that. I felt a tremendous burden being lifted. Light coming into my darkness. Oh, I was so very hopeful.

Josh wanted to attend seminary at Regent College in Vancouver and be closer to his family on the West Coast. It made sense for him to prepare for a meaningful career. But I hoped we could both benefit from this opportunity for change.

In our old paradigm, as the supportive wife, this would mean that I should support him while he got his master's degree. We would have no income while he was in school. He wasn't requiring that of me, but still I felt the pressure of expectations set long ago. The role I played in my family, the way my husband and kids saw me, the way I saw myself. These things were deeply etched into our way of living. If I was going to break away from these expectations I wanted him truly behind me. But I kept bumping up against an invisible partition. It felt like I was on one side of it with the house and the children, and he was on the other side with the rest of the world.

I was beginning to see double standards everywhere. For instance, spending money on career training, projects, and education was considered a worthwhile investment for him in a way that it wasn't for me. Conversations about what he wanted for the future led to changes in our reality, while conversations about what I wanted for the future remained as conversations.

I started speaking up more, and this was causing tension between us. We had a silly argument that grew to epic proportions over the choice of a new car for me. In the end I got what I wanted, but I'm not sure how high a price I paid for it in terms of my relationship.

In relationships, the holy rule in our church had been men socialized with men, women socialized with women, and married couples with married couples. Married men having friendships with other women was off limits and vice versa. Josh disregarded that rule when he pursued friendships with two women. We spent a lot of time with them together, and I enjoyed their company. He would occasionally spend time with them alone. There was no infidelity. But if our roles had been reversed? If I had been the one pursuing a friendship with another man, single or married? I could not imagine a scenario where that would have gone over very well. And yet, there we were.

Clearly, I was finding my voice and seeing the double standard we had been living all these years. The more I asserted my wants and desires, the more I realized I was not being taken seriously. I didn't feel supported with anything outside of the wife-and-mother box. My husband was not willing to entertain the idea of me pursuing my own career unless it held direct benefit for him or our family. He was not willing to work through details that might help me reach my goals as well as his. Sure, it would be hard for both of us, but we could do it.

The foundation of our marriage was being tested—the structure, the strength, the depth. We were entering new territory. Could our marriage support the needs of both people in it or did it only work in its current form? Would this man be willing to accompany me where *I* wanted to go? I wasn't so sure.

leaving oz.

IT WAS MAY, and I was feeling strange when I drove through the state park up to the pavilion for the staff picnic. I almost stayed home on a fake excuse. We'd gotten word that our request for a six-month sabbatical was denied. We were offered three months, but I wasn't willing to stay for three. As it turned out, this would be my last staff picnic.

Everyone who kept the church running, from the pastors to the building staff and all their children and babies, were there. There were plastic red-checked tablecloths and large aluminum servers of fried chicken, hot dogs, hamburgers, and coleslaw. I used to look forward to these picnics.

I was standing in the food line when another pastor's wife standing in front of me asked me how I was. We hadn't spoken in some time, and out of all the women on the team, I would say I knew her the least. I looked at her in the eye, searching to see if she was wanting a real answer or not. I couldn't tell.

I'd been giving the same fake answer for years now. The upbeat, positive answer that you give no matter how devastatingly crappy you feel. I decided whether she wanted a real answer or not, she was getting one. The past few years had been *really, really* hard, I said. The publicity, the scandals, the split, the loss of friendships, the online critics—all of it. I was hurt, angry, and exhausted. When she didn't say much, I turned to get some chicken.

A few weeks later I was in the lobby after the service. It was thick with people, and as usual I stopped to have several conversations before gathering up my kids and going home. I had only a few Sundays left at the church.

Out of the corner of my eye I saw the same woman from the picnic heading directly for me from the other side of the lobby. When she arrived in front of me she asked if she could speak to me for a moment. (Again, just tell the person you don't have any moments!) In the past I would have braced myself for whatever criticism was coming, but this time I felt none of the usual anxiety. As she began to challenge me about my complaining attitude at the picnic, I didn't even care. I guess the counseling had set me free.

In fact, as I was leaving the building that afternoon I laughed, thanking her in my head. I couldn't have planned a more fitting ending to this chapter of my life. *I have been wrong since I got here, and I am still wrong now.*

Part Five

EXODUS

canada.

ON THE PLANE from Baltimore to Vancouver I breathed a wonderful, glorious, and deep sigh of relief.

Vancouver would be a new beginning for us, for my family and for me. I wouldn't have to be anything to anyone anymore. No one would be watching us. I wouldn't even have to talk to anyone if I didn't want to. I wouldn't have to uphold laws that someone else made. I wouldn't have to eat, sleep, and sit in a stew that someone else made twenty years ago and left for me to find festering in a dark corner. We could put all of it behind us. Maybe?

bright eyes.

WE MOVED TO Vancouver so Josh could attend Regent College, a school of theology located on the coast of British Columbia, Canada. Originally from the West Coast, he was eager to return. There were other theology schools to which he applied. But those schools were affiliated closely with specific church denominations, which was not appealing to either of us. We both wanted a broader perspective. We'd heard Regent had a bit of a reputation for causing a crisis of faith in people.

All of the drama of the last few years of church had left me feeling disillusioned. Personally, I couldn't wait to have a crisis of faith. Since we'd only just arrived in Vancouver and I had few friends or connections, I got involved at Regent. That semester I audited a class, joined a lunch discussion group, and attended evening lectures that interested me. Josh and I were fortunate to be invited by a few of the professors to their homes for dinner. The professors' beliefs were varied—some Catholic, some Protestant, some Orthodox, and best of all, some were women.

The spirit of Regent was like the first spring after many winters. I finally felt myself relax. There was no performance necessary. Here, I could just *be.* Compared to the right-wrong, black-white world I'd come from, Regent was an invitation to think differently. It was a place for sharing ideas and open discussion and learning new things. A little community of its own.

At Regent, questions and differing opinions were encouraged and expected. Professors didn't focus all their energy on convincing or defending a particular view, they just taught their specialty. No one was trying to be right. I felt like I had finally landed back on the planet I had come from, the one where people were free to do the things that regular humans do—like *think*, for starters.

So I began thinking.

Believe it or not, I was still wrestling over the issue of women in leadership and teaching roles. The men at church had built a strong, high wall of theological arguments that kept women out of the pulpit, out of most leadership positions, and even out of careers. For so long this wall and all of their reasons felt indestructible, unquestionable, and immoveable. But then one afternoon I had lunch with Madison. Madison was a graduate student and the admissions counselor at Regent. I was asking her what she wanted to do once she finished her master's degree. She was talking about her love for people and how much she wanted to become the pastor of a quaint, rural town somewhere in the British countryside. As she said this, an image of her walking green landscape in Wellington boots popped into my mind. Her eyes lit up with sparkles as she talked about it and she was just radiating positive energy. It was the same spark I had when I thought about music or performing.

After that day I started thinking a lot about the light in Madison's eyes as she spoke about her dreams for the future. What was the point of being alive if not to find things that spark our souls into aliveness? Wasn't that why we are all here? Why had the church worked so hard to limit the interests and passions of women? Weren't there better uses of church time and finances? Like caring for orphans or feeding the hungry or rescuing girls from human trafficking? Why would anyone want to keep someone like Madison from pastoring in any community, anywhere? I imagined all the people who would miss out on being loved by her charming, radiating spirit. If God wanted to squash women's dreams so badly, God could handle it.

One sunny day a few weeks later I was walking out the front doors of Regent and I climbed over that wall of theological authority. That wall had been built by powerful, influential men. Men with PhDs, big audiences, and lots of money flowing through their ministries. Men who wrote thick, heady books, some of whom I'd even eaten lunch with. I didn't care anymore if these men had a thousand reasons on paper why they thought they were right. I had one living reason for why I *knew* I was right. Bright eyes. I thought if God was in anything at all it had to be sparkling, bright eyes.

rabbit hutch.

I NAMED THE house the Rabbit Hutch because the basement was so dank it reminded me of a root cellar, and that made me think of carrots and potatoes and rabbits.

A few months before this, before we'd moved in, we needed to register our children in person for school, and so we stopped by to see the rental house we'd be living in. (The one I had insisted on renting online in advance.) From the outside there was potential. A mature garden, a pretty stone walkway, and a deck. But stepping inside, my heart sunk to the floor.

There was only one proper bathroom. The second bathroom was dangerous. The master bedroom had only one small window I could barely see out of, and some of the storage spaces were dirty, damp, and difficult to access. Most importantly there was the aura. I don't know if you feel auras, but apparently I do and this aura wasn't good. And any other year, a no-good aura might have been fine. But this year a no-good aura was not fine. It was definitely not fine. I needed love. Rest. Creativity. Psychotherapy. Closets. My own bathroom. With an outlet.

I hoped the house would prove me wrong.

fog.

THE VANCOUVER WINTER arrived with its customary fog, rain, and early dark evenings, which matched my insides perfectly. The initial excitement of the move had worn off and the kids were settled in to their new schools and routines. And I was faced with some realities. One, I was still depressed. Two, my brain was foggy. But not regular foggy. It was heavy foggy. Like there was an enormous boulder in my brain taking up nearly all the good, usable space.

I started the year taking long, daily walks, moving in slow motion. Most days I couldn't think about anything because of the boulder. But one particular day I saw another picture in my mind. (You may remember the first one, where I'm the gnarly old beggar woman.)

This time I was sitting alone in a dim and sterile room with cement floors and high ceilings. There was a heavy door with a metal door-knob that was shut. I was in the middle, on the floor, and all around me were disorderly stacks of manila file folders of various heights. I was going through the stacks and folders one by one searching for something, only I didn't know what. I just knew that when I came upon it, I would immediately know that it was the thing I'd been looking for.

The thing, of course, was me. I hadn't seen the whole me in seventeen years since I abandoned her in the weeks leading up to my wedding day. I had ignored many parts of myself to make myself fit what the church had asked of me. If anything, it was surprising I didn't notice her absence earlier.

But as the children got settled in their schools and my husband got busy with his classes and making new friends, I found myself with fewer commitments, fewer expectations, and fewer relationships than ever before. I was completely disconnected from the mother church that had so fiercely insisted I hold a certain shape. That life was gone now, and it was strange how removed from it I was in every way. Now I felt formless. And despite the fact that I couldn't locate myself, I was more naked and exposed than ever. In a way, there was nothing here *except* me.

• • •

> *For centuries, men have projected their inner image of femininity, raising it to a consciousness that [leaves] women who [accept] the projection separated from their own reality.*
>
> Marion Woodman, *Leaving My Father's House*

patti and cate.

PATTI HIRED ME for a pet-sitting job. We needed the money, but honestly, I was just doing it to get out of the house. And I wanted to make sure I could still relate to humankind. The address she gave me was just a few streets over. When I rang the doorbell for our meeting, a spunky woman in her fifties with tanned skin, spikey brown hair, and a husky voice opened the door. She was the kind of woman you knew had a tattoo somewhere and a slew of stories to tell. She invited me in to meet her cats, Fred and Max. Orange and gray, respectively. She and her partner, Cate, loved to travel, and they were going away for a few days.

It worked out so well that Patti hired me again for their next trip. The next thing I knew, she was inviting me over for coffee. We started talking music, and when she said she had a keen ear I told her about the songs I was writing. She wanted to hear them, so I played her a few rough sketches of songs I was working on. Afterward, she told me she thought I was holding back and that she wanted to hear me really let go.

I was surprised.

One, that she cared to hear it at all. Two, that she was really listening. She barely knew me, and she already had me pegged. Was it that obvious? She was right, I felt trapped inside myself. The church hadn't exactly been a safe environment for self-expression.

Over that first coffee and a few more subsequent ones I told her about my life as a pastor's wife and how we came to move to Vancouver. She listened intently, occasionally stopping to handroll a cigarette and stand half-outside the back kitchen door to smoke it. She told me about her younger, wilder days, organizing music for parties, living rough in South America somewhere, about past boyfriends and girlfriends.

Cate was taller, blonde, with a proper British accent. She was easygoing and relaxed. The kind of person who melts the stress off you if you just stand near enough. Despite Cate having a high-profile job, she was unassuming and savvy. An intellectual, she always had a book going.

Coffee turned into another coffee, which turned into dinner, which turned into dinners with family, dinner with friends, which turned into girls' nights.

Our first girls' night was easily the most fun I'd had in years. Chinese food, IPA beers for Patti and Cate, wine for me, and shots for everyone after that. Patti had a bell she kept on her kitchen island, the kind you ring for service at a counter. Anytime anybody wanted more wine or beer they would ring the bell and somebody else would pour it. Just when I thought the night was almost over, Patti slipped to the next room for a second and returned with three shot glasses and some Croatian brandy I now call evil. They walked me home that night, the three of us linked in arms, laughing and singing like drunken sailors.

• • •

One evening over dinner Cate asked me straight up what I thought about their lesbian relationship.

It put me on the spot, but by this time I had a hunch our friendship wasn't hanging on the balance of my answer. Months earlier it seemed that we had accepted one another as is. Still, it was not an easy question to answer. The answer I'd been saying for the past twenty years as a churchgoer was the usual *God loves all people, but the plan for marriage was for men and women.*

That answer is easy to give when the only people you interact with believe what you believe, when you only spend time with people exactly like yourself. It's a very different thing to say those words to your friends, who you love, who love each other, whose kitchen you are standing in, while eating Chinese food they bought for you.

I did give that answer that day, but as I mumbled the words I realized I didn't believe them anymore. Patti and Cate loved each other, and it made me happy to see them happy. They had taught me something new about love and it was that love, in any form, is a good thing.

dogma.

I HOPED THAT moving to a new city was going to bring my husband and me closer together. And I had assumed the disconnectedness I felt in my marriage was due to our busy schedule and the craziness of the previous few years. Instead, I didn't recognize my marriage here. It wasn't inflated with importance here. We weren't famous or special. We weren't needing to uphold the laws of someone else's kingdom. We were just two ordinary people. More than a few times I looked at Josh, cocked my head to the side, and thought, *Wait, do I know you?*

Beliefs and principles we'd spent years of our life upholding were slipping away with no acknowledgment or fanfare, and it made me angry, since I'd exhausted myself upholding these ideas. For instance, kids and communion. Our church wanted children to wait to take communion until they were old enough to make a profession of faith. Before then, it was discouraged. When my children were young and would ask why they could not take communion, I struggled to make sense of this for them. It felt like I was saying, *Well, honey, Jesus died for everyone, but for some people we need to see some proof of ID first.* It just didn't sound right coming out of my mouth.

My daughter and I must have had a hundred bedtime conversations where she would share her fears about her faith with me. She was so afraid that she wouldn't reach or attain this proof that our religion insisted was the one and only sign of true faith. She was anxious she would never come to believe the same things as her own family. I hated to watch her struggle in this way, and at the same time I loved her honesty.

Fast-forward to some random church in Vancouver we've visited maybe three times, and out of nowhere their dad tells the kids to go ahead and take communion because it's fine. *It's fine?* I felt gut punched. I had held her off for fourteen years because she was supposed to be "born again" and all of a sudden that didn't matter? My daughter was confused and angry.

That wasn't the only place where the rules seemed to change overnight. The issue of women and work was another one that I couldn't just brush off. This was *the* defining feature of our church back home and the reason I set my dreams down on a block of cold ice.

But when my husband began suggesting it would be a good idea for me to get a part-time job, I felt an intense anger rise up in me instantly. Each time we'd end up in a circular argument headed for nowhere. It wasn't that I was against working or helping. I was against changing on a dime, beliefs that had come at great cost to me without a note of appreciation or an acknowledgment that we were ditching them. What happened to "This is a God-ordained belief" signed by Jesus in red-blood ink? Now that we needed the money, God was suddenly willing to renegotiate the terms?

These beliefs had cost me dearly. I'd been "busy at home" our entire married life. I'd modeled this kind of wife to thousands of women. I had given so much of myself to be the woman they wanted and I wouldn't, I couldn't pretend that it didn't matter.

kindling.

WHEN I WAS little kid my dad loved to build a fire on winter evenings. He'd send me and my brother out into the yard to collect the thinnest sticks we could find, and when we got back he'd be crumpling newspaper into loose, long rolls and placing them under the grate. Then he'd add the kindling we'd collected and the logs. One of the newspaper rolls would be lit like a torch and he'd let me hold it up the chimney to get the air flowing upward. Then he'd light one of the newspaper rolls under the grate and the magical progression upward would begin. The match would light the newspaper, the newspaper would light the kindling, and the kindling would light the logs. An hour later we'd be sprawled out in front of the fire like cats, melting in the warmth and the heat that we'd made. I think that's what we are supposed to be as women—so filled with the heat and warmth of our own fire that we never go cold. Tending to our fire to see that it never goes out. And if it does happen to go out it's okay. We start over. We gather the things we need to build our fire again and then light a match under it.

That was what I was doing when I signed up for music classes at the local community college. It wasn't really where I wanted to be, but it was an attempt to go out and find some newspaper and sticks at least. I was gathering kindling. I was also doing it so I wouldn't look like the depressed wife that I was and more like someone who was too busy to take a part-time job. At least this way I would have time to work on the fire. I figured if I had homework in the evenings like my kids, I would clearly be too busy to get a job. My plan worked.

At school some magic happened. I wrote my first composition. It was a baby's composition, but it was mine.

By chance I happened to meet a young violinist, and I had her come to the house and record the piece for me. A few months later I met a master violinist at a small church I was attending, and I mentioned the piece in passing, since it happened to be for violin and piano. He asked me to send it to him, and a few days later wrote back offering to include it in his upcoming concert, even giving me the option of having the whole orchestra play it. I was thrilled! A few weeks later I was taking a bow in front of two hundred people as the composer of this piece that had just been performed. It was a dream come true. My music brought to life just because one person heard what I was saying with it and liked it.

To think I'd been stuck inside that church where a simple moment like this never would have happened for me. This was something I had wanted for as long as I could remember—to not just deliver the music of others but to create my own and be seen and acknowledged more wholly as a musician. The fact that my piece had been recognized by this talented, accomplished person was almost bewildering. I realized then that all that time I had only needed to open the door of my cage and stick my damn foot out.

It's not surprising that a woman would go looking for herself in a place she naturally feels most connected to herself. A woman's creativity is intimately connected to her vitality and flourishing. Creating something from our own heart or hands is important to our sense of self-worth. It gives us opportunities to learn. It allows us to see ourselves in new ways and be seen and recognized by others. Every person needs that.

the galápagos islands.

WHEN I WAS little girl my grandmother Mums, the photographer-explorer one, used to give us evening slide shows whenever she came back from one of her exotic trips. She had her photos turned into small square slides she would drop into a circular projector that moved one place over whenever she clicked a button. I was more interested in the projector than her photos because the projector made this great sound whenever the button was pressed, but more importantly because a photograph of the Galápagos Islands is not the Galápagos Islands. In comparison to the real thing, a photograph is flat and one-dimensional and it couldn't hold my interest. Which is precisely how it can feel when you are trying to live out a projection of someone that is not really you. You feel flat and one-dimensional because you are flat and one-dimensional. And because in order to be something that you're not, you have to deny all the wonderful things that you are.

As I began to find my own identity again, I remembered. Being myself isn't nearly as exhausting as being somebody I am not. The "biblical woman" was not a real woman, she was a picture, a projection, a product! A man-made product, literally. An ideal to achieve. You can order whole books on Amazon and become her too. But she wasn't me and she wasn't tons of women. She was the woman they wanted. That's all. The woman *they* wanted.

It was like wearing an outfit, though women might all wear her a little differently. Some women slung her over their shoulder, wearing just enough to pass approval. Some threw her down and left. Some women, like me, got completely lost in her. I could wear this woman, but that didn't mean I was this woman.

These men had no clue who I really was on the inside.

This was a model of convenience. Having women cast to the side of business affairs, keeping them busy with children and homekeeping tasks? It meant that men didn't have to share their spaces. Or change their plan or stop to discuss. It meant they could still receive the credit. It meant they could maintain their position of power and authority in the home and in the church.

And for women? What did it mean for them? How does it help society for a woman to live as a mere fraction of herself? What if Barbara Streisand never sang? What if Julia Child never went to France to study cooking? Had these women been in my church, their talents never would have seen the light of day. How many Barbaras and Julias are out there quietly shrinking instead of growing?

You wouldn't expect a honeybee to only perform part of its function or a whale to thrive for years in a pen. And yet this is what some churches do to women. If women were fish it would be like saying, "Look here, lady fishes, we don't care what kind of fish you are, you are all going to live as trout." They are expecting women to thrive while attempting to fulfill a generic and limited identity. Or only part of their identity. What a waste. What a senseless waste.

When I accepted the church's name for me, I lost my power and vivacity and authenticity because their name for me wasn't true. They reduced my identity to wife, mother, and singer. Yes, I am those things, but I am also many other things. I am also an individual with opinions and ideas. I'm a communicator and an artist. When any person is deliberately limited because of their gender, race, sexuality, and so on, bells and sirens should be going off in our minds.

I understand better now the rebellious teen or the adult who was once all in and suddenly disappears without a word. This is often the most authentic person in the bunch. This is the person saying, "I won't be this person you want me to be. I am not playing this game of pretend." To choose to leave the box—the tradition of church or family—is to do something brave. This is the person who is risking respect, connection, and security to become their true selves. The church needs people like this who question norms and seek independence. Blindly following the leader is unhealthy and the entire group can be harmed.

This is part of what makes a woman's journey so incredible and so treacherous. To become our own, most of us cannot just create something from scratch. We have to reject something first. We might have to leave a structure that feels safe and right to us and venture into the unknown to become ourselves. Is it any wonder many women never do venture there? It seems like there is no map to follow. But when we refuse to let other people name us, a healthy vacuum is created. If no one else is allowed to name us, then we will have to name ourselves. If a woman won't be who her father tells her to be, or who her husband tells her to be, or who her culture tells her to be, who will she be instead?

• • •

So long as a woman accepts a man's archetypal projection, she is trapped in a male understanding of reality.

Marion Woodman, *Leaving My Father's House*

vodka tonic.

AND SO I chose a new name for myself. Although even then the name I chose was too limiting. It takes time to stretch out, to expand, to be more of yourself. Because when you've been living in a man-centric world where a woman's needs matter less than those of her husband and children, making changes to this arrangement is considerably harder than it looks. People are used to the niceties that you provide. You know, things like dinner and free childcare.

What I would have loved was for my husband to reach across to me and release me of all the *shoulds* still swirling in my head. *I should get a part-time job. I should save our family from draining our savings. I should support my husband while he gets his master's degree.* Instead, I put pressure on myself to bring in a salary. Some of that pressure was my own and some was the problem of inequality and worth in my marriage, which was still unresolved.

The evening I called my mother to tell her I was *not* going to pursue my music but that I'd applied and been accepted into a teaching program, her anger on the other end of the line was palpable and it caught my attention. This was a tone I'd heard only once before in the last twenty years, and that time happened to be the day she suggested I not stay involved at the church. I was about to betray myself again, and she knew it and I knew it and we both knew that we both knew it. I got off the phone quickly and slunk to my room.

Ah, my mother. All that I owe that woman.

I would have to be a fool to ignore her again. She was right, I did not really want to be a teacher. *Okay. To hell with the shoulds*, I thought. Life is not martyrdom. It is not burning yourself for others until you turn to cold ashes and die, and people at your funeral exclaim what a wonderful woman you were. Meanwhile your dreams never saw the light of day. No. That is not respect for a woman's life, that is a waste of it.

I would pursue the music. For my mother. And for myself. And so that one day I wouldn't be an eighty-year-old woman dressed in elegant black staring out from an upstairs window holding a vodka tonic in her hand wishing just once she had stepped beyond the wall of her fears to see what lay on the other side.

the gift of kindness.

I WAS HALF-EXPECTING Asa to laugh at me when I contacted him out of the blue to tell him I was trying to reinvent myself at forty-something. Asa was a musician friend I'd known growing up and I contacted him hoping he might have some connections in the music business. The last time we spoke we were just kids. He didn't laugh, and that surprised me. Then I expected him to talk for an hour about all that he knew and all he had done and what I should do and how I should do it. But he didn't do that either, and that surprised me too.

It took me five whole minutes to send him the first song I ever wrote. I hadn't shared my music with anyone before. He was waiting for it on the other end of the line while I stared at my phone, too scared to press *send.*

"What are you doing?" he asked.

"I'm staring at my phone," I replied. "I'm afraid to send it."

"The world needs to hear your music, Shannon," he urged.

I thought about it for a few moments and then pressed *send.* Then I waited for his response.

"Ever Since We Said Goodbye." It is a song about feeling lost after leaving the church and waiting for change. I didn't want to be back there. But sometimes I missed it anyway. Finally his text came through.

"Shannon," he said. "It feels like coming home."

He was right. I was coming home. Because music is home for me. Despite all the music I had done with the church, I had still managed to become separated with this part of myself. It was the church's music I was connected to, not mine. Always their vision, never my vision. Always their dreams, never my dreams.

Maybe it was because he already knew me, or because we shared similar dreams for our lives, or maybe it was because he just simply cared. I don't know. But I was seen, and in being seen for some reason I felt permission to see myself again.

Running into Asa was like hitting a brick wall of kindness. The good and the hurt smacked me at the same time. What I was getting from Asa illuminated what had been missing. There was a sense of memory about it—I was remembering life before church and the way I lived in the world and the way the world responded to me. I realized I had become invisible in my own life. I had been in a holding pattern for so long—frozen, stuck, unmoving, unfeeling—it had all come to feel so normal. But it wasn't normal. It wasn't normal to feel this way at all.

I remembered something else, too. I remembered that love should feel like love. Whether it is friendship love or God's love or parental love or spousal love it doesn't matter. Love should feel like love. If it feels like something less, then it probably is.

the work.

TO WRITE THE music I was forced to be honest with myself. My music became my truth telling. My truth telling became my music. It was how I began to create a new identity for myself. *I am something different than what you people said. Let me try to tell you who I think I am.* This was the hard work I had avoided all those years ago—looking deep within me and bringing out the person I knew I was. All my old fears were still there, along with some new ones. I now know what happens when you avoid the work you are supposed to do. By work I don't mean a job title, I'm talking about the work of bringing your authentic self out into the world.

It wasn't made any easier for the fact that I'd spent far too long sitting on the bench. I felt like a child because I was still a child. When life is dictated to you by others saying *be this, do that, stand here*, it's as if they draw lines and cages around you emotionally, physically, intellectually, and spiritually. There is no safe place to try, fail, or even experiment in that kind of environment. There is no way to learn to lead yourself. I had grown accustomed to standing on the periphery of my own life *watching other people live.* We have to push past those boundaries in order to grow.

There were negative attitudes I had to squash having to do with women being selfish to put themselves forward or making themselves noticed. I was so out of practice doing this. Every time I shared something from my deeper self, like a song or a poem or even an opinion, I waged a miniwar inside me. Even my body was stuck in old patterns, proof that our beliefs become physical. One time I was trying to speak, and I noticed even my jaw was resistant to moving. Here I was, a trained singer and performer with a degree in communication, and the act of speaking out loud had become agonizing. It was painful, but I kept stepping through my fear and every time I did I noticed it got a tiny bit easier and I got a tiny bit braver.

The more I stepped out of the old me and into myself, the more I saw the falseness of the identity the men at church had designed for me. No wonder I had felt invisible.

The real me was coming out from a dark womb where I'd been hidden all this time. This was the seed that for all these years sat in me unwatered, unfertilized. The seed was me! And just like in physical birth, there was difficulty and fear. And a lot of it. It was a rite of passage. I realized I was going to have to push myself out into the world inch by inch. It was scary, it was exhilarating. I wanted to go, I wanted to stop, it was always two steps forward and one step back. My husband and children could watch, but they couldn't understand or do this work. I had to do this alone.

The work looks different for every woman, every person. But it is loving and nurturing ourselves. It's watering the seeds that live inside us. And letting them grow and reach the light. We are making something unseen seen. It's a common pitfall for a young woman to avoid this work. We delay because we think there is plenty of time or because there are fears about the unknown, or we don't know how to do it, or we get caught up in somebody else's work, mistaking it for our own. Had I stayed in the church, I would never have done this. So there are traps that will keep a woman from becoming herself. Traps outside us and traps in our own minds. Almost anything will sound easier than doing this work. Some women spend their entire lives avoiding this work by finding other, less vulnerable work to do. Anything but facing her deepest fears and strongest longings. Anything but risking failure or embarrassment. Anything but going it alone.

But this is exactly the work that we need to do. Believing our seeds matter, facing our fears, and finding our courage. Our authentic self is the most difficult self to bring out into the light because the stakes are so high. We are exposed if it is the real us.

How can a woman become herself when so much of her is kept hidden? She cannot. Our seeds held in darkness cannot not grow. But with love, and care, and attention and nurturing and time, they can.

• • •

> *Living by principles is not living your own life. It is easier to try to be better than you are than to be who you are. If you are trying to live by ideals, you are constantly plagued by a sense of unreality. Somewhere you think there must be some joy; it can't be all "must," "ought to," "have to." And when the crunch comes, you have to recognize the truth: you weren't there.*
>
> Marion Woodman, *Addiction to Perfection*

dreams.

THE STUDIO WHERE I was to record my album looked as though it hadn't been dusted in a few years. A huge drum set took up most of the front room on a rug. Organs, guitars, and framed awards lined the walls, but I was only interested in the piano. A walnut-colored Steinway took up the corner by the front window. I walked over to it and pressed the keys. The piano was old. It was the kind of piano that stays slightly out of tune no matter what you do. For a split second I panicked as I realized what this meant for my music. My album was going to sound like the 1970s. Whatever. This project was more about getting myself to this moment than it was about the actual music.

The sun shined down on me that whole week, and this time I was the one with bright eyes. In fact, brighter eyes on a girl have never been seen since. I was my old self again. I was giddy. I was bouncy. As I waited for the bus to take me to the studio each morning, I could not help but think about how I had gotten there and why. I stopped waiting for someone to give me permission.

the year I sat in bed.

THE YEAR KATE SPADE killed herself I was spending most of my time in my room sitting on my bed, which meant I was facing the back of my bedroom door. It just happened to have a sturdy gold hook on it. I'd stare at that hook and wonder if it was strong enough to hold me if I decided to kill myself. I thought to myself *I get it, Kate. I really do.* My spine was curling from sitting so much. I took naps just to forget how miserable I felt, and many mornings I was disappointed to learn I had woken up. Dying honestly sounded easier than facing the future.

You see, while it was wonderful to have finally had a positive upturn in events by having reconnected with my identity and my purpose, it was these events that shook me wide awake. Those were the very things I'd lost while I was busy "obeying" the church! I had just spent nearly twenty years trying to meet someone else's standards. Twenty years fulfilling someone else's dream. I felt robbed. And this was just the tip of the iceberg. If I could lose these parts of myself that were so very important, because the church insisted I do so, I had to wonder, *What other parts of me had been lost?*

Then there was my marriage to face. I hadn't found my identity and purpose within my marriage, I found these things because I put on my muck boots and trudged alone outside my everyday life to get them and bring them back. Inside my marriage, I had done all the things I knew to do. And still there was no future for me. I had learned to live without the things I needed and I didn't want to go on like this anymore.

The questions I was asking were the same ones anybody might ask after waking up from a long, unconscious sleep. *Where am I? How did I get here?*

I decided I needed to understand my own story. I needed to know how a bright, capable woman from a good and loving family could end up so far removed from herself as I had. So I did what anyone in my situation might do. I went back to the beginning. I pulled the covers up over my head with the one creature who I was certain loved me. My cat. And I spent the year searching for answers.

Part Six

MISSING PIECES

the cost of the trade.

THE FIRST REVELATION I had the year I sat in bed was that I had made a deal without realizing it when I entered the church and when I married my husband—a deal with patriarchy, if you will. And while I had upheld my end of it, the men I'd made the deal with had not upheld theirs.

They wanted me to submit and follow, and I did. I'd embraced their ideas, and I'd done my part of the work. I stayed at home, supported my husband, and raised the children. I'd gotten up every morning and tried my best to fulfill patriarchy's dreams—the dream of male leadership. In return, the men of the church had promised to protect and love me. But they did not do that.

They did not protect or cherish me. They did not acknowledge the whole me. How can someone protect or cherish something they don't even see? Or don't wish to see? I had no voice or place in their world. The real me was punished and tamed like Eve, and the only acceptable version of me was a woman resembling the Virgin Mary dressed in twenty-first-century clothing. All the parts of me, the parts of a woman that lay somewhere in between Mary and Eve, the beautiful things that make a woman feel vibrant and alive—her mind, her body, her spirit, her dreams, her freedom, her endless possibilities—those parts were stamped in bold, red capital lettering: DENIED. The church protected a woman all right, but it was not me. It was the ghost of a woman.

Then I thought about my husband. He wanted me without my past, so I threw my ring into the sea. He wanted me to marry him without my dear friends by my side, so I left them behind too. I felt overlooked many times since then, and I finally understood why. He married me, but without ever having accepted me or respecting me first. In fact, he never agreed to marry the real, whole me. He agreed to marry a small part of me. A shrunken version of me.

As my thoughts solidified I stared at the wall in front of me. A mixture of regret, disappointment, anger, and shame washed over me as I took in the depth of their meaning. I wasn't sure which realization was worse. The fact that the church failed to love and protect me, the fact that my husband failed to love and protect me, or the fact that I had failed to love and protect me.

After that, I wept. For the friends I lost. For the women and men back at church who I knew were still hurting and disillusioned. For my marriage, which I wasn't sure would or could survive. But most of all, I wept for myself. I wept for the nine-year-old child whose parents told her they were separating. I wept for the teen who was afraid to pursue her dream of becoming a singer. I wept for the young woman who fell in love with a famous preacher and thought with faith she could do what her parents couldn't. I wept for the wife who tried to be perfect in every way the church wanted her to be. I wept for my children and the mother who required absolute obedience from her children because that is what the church asked of her. I wept for the woman inside me who never found the courage to be who she really was.

• • •

Each of us must recognize where we have cooperated with our own oppression.

Christiane Northrup, *Women's Bodies, Women's Wisdom*

nothingness.

THE OCEAN HAS always been my soul place. I can almost feel my messy self being scrubbed sea-salt clean. Or rocked by the gentle waves. Sometimes, on extra good days I would go down to the water to sit with the ocean in the hopes that my foggy mind would be made clear. The curves of the shoreline, the waters rolling in and receding back, the movement, the rhythm all reminding me that life is an endless cycle of comings and goings, here and gone, here and gone. Still, I did not know what to do.

My world felt vast and lonely and empty. I didn't know a life could be so very full and noisy and then so very quiet. *Nothingness* is how I would have described it if someone had asked. I wanted to get the empty feeling over with and out of me. I hated the foggy feeling of depression. But it wasn't up to me. I would listen to my body and let it lead the way. It was clearly not rushing through this. I had years of bottled-up feelings inside and at times they felt as heavy as bags of stones.

We often think life is linear until something happens to remind us that it is not. Life is cyclical. Nature shows us this. We are part of the natural world, but so often I think we forget it. We think there is something wrong with us if we cannot forever maintain a certain trajectory upward. In work, in relationships—in anything. We are hard on those who appear unproductive—the little ones, the aged, the weak—instead of aware of their special brilliance and wisdom. We have this idea that we are supposed to be always moving up and up or always producing, and that is not how life works. Even a beautiful flower dies off and gets ugly. It is a mistake to value only the moment of flowering. The times of growth and dying off and nothingness are just as important. It is in these times we can learn the most.

In nothingness you can hear yourself think in a way that you couldn't before. Gone are the opinions and voices and directives of others, and having time like this is a necessity. It is easy to lose sight of who you are and why you are alive when someone is always talking in your ear.

It was there in the stillness and quiet that I began to find the missing pieces. *My* missing pieces. Like a woman walking along the beach among the shells, one by one I came upon my own glistening bits. A bit of my truth here, a small piece of my worth there. Important parts of me that had gotten lost in the ocean of men's voices and clapping and loud hymns. Once I found the first few I just knew there had to be more. I was determined to find them all.

twilight sleep.

MY MOTHER DOESN'T remember anything about my brother's birth because she birthed under twilight sleep, the method of childbirth used by most hospitals in the US in 1970. In fact, I can recall asking her about having babies when I was a little girl and finding her answers strangely vague, as if she hadn't been there. It turns out this was true in a way. Her vague response reflected her removed experience.

Just after the turn of the century wealthy women were asking for a way to have a less painful childbirth, and doctors were looking for a solution in response to their requests. A couple of German obstetricians discovered a particular mixture of drugs that allowed a woman to enter a state of quasi-sleep during labor and delivery and wake up when it was all over with a baby in her arms, remembering next to nothing of the experience. They called it twilight sleep.

Women were elated. Have a baby with less pain and suffering? Word spread quickly as women talked about it in their kitchens and neighborhoods. Influential women used it and spoke positively about their experiences. Women's magazines popularized it. Soon it was the birth method of choice for the privileged in America and it stayed that way for more than half a century.

Twilight sleep drastically changed our ideas and perceptions about birth. For example, before twilight sleep birthing was seen as a natural occurrence of a woman's body. Women usually gave birth at home supported by caring women and midwives. During birth a woman could eat, drink, and move around freely. The woman giving birth was the one in the room with the most information about what was happening; she was the expert in the room. And regardless of the birth's outcome, one thing is for certain—she got the full experience.

After twilight sleep, the perception of birth shifted from a natural event to a medical procedure. Medical students learned about birth in textbooks alongside illnesses and diseases. Because of the heavy drugs used in twilight sleep, birthing was moved into the hospital in case something were to go wrong. Instead of the birth mother being the most knowledgeable person in the room, the doctor was. Instead of having the freedom to move and respond to her body, a woman was confined to a bed and sometimes constrained with straps. Her eyes and ears were wrapped in gauze to dull her senses and then she was placed in a dark room where she might labor for hours on end alone, barely conscious.

At first, only positive stories were shared. But eventually, women began to recall their experiences and the darker picture emerged. Many women suffered severe lacerations from the straps and thrashing during hallucinations. There were traumatic episodes of psychosis with head banging, screaming, and other forms of self-harm. Women lay alone for hours, neglected, sometimes soiled in their own vomit and feces. Babies were born barely breathing or not at all, and sometimes injured by forceps. Many women awakened to find they felt no recognition of their baby or connection to the birth.

• • •

With all due respect to the doctors who invented twilight sleep in response to the requests of women, the birth was no longer about the woman and her experience. It was about the doctor who was standing over her and the artificial experience he was creating on her behalf. Birthing, but with the mother's own presence removed from the event. Is it any wonder the woman wakes up later feeling disconnected from it? From herself? From her baby?

I can't help but imagine a mother in the hospital the morning after the birth. She is sitting in bed holding her baby when the doctor walks in and says to her while looking down at his papers, "You had a wonderful birth last night." He exchanges a quick glance with the nurse who attended the mother the night before. The mother slowly looks down at her baby, trying to remember the birth but finds herself coming up blank. She wonders, *Was it wonderful?*

This story feels familiar, only instead of a physical birth I'm thinking of a spiritual birth. My spiritual birth. I was a young woman wanting to know more about God. I would have done just fine on my own, but I went into the church because that was where the God experts were. I entrusted myself to them. But rather than work with me on this, they took over and excluded me and so reduced my awareness and participation in an experience that was supposed to be mine. And I wonder, how much of my life have I missed while the men were busy directing it?

• • •

> *Most modern civilizations are characterized by the belief that intellect is superior to emotions, the mind and spirit are superior to and entirely separate from the body, masculinity is superior to femininity, and nature is something to be exploited for her resources.*
>
> Christiane Northrup, *Women's Bodies, Women's Wisdom*

my wisdom, my knowing.

MY KNOWING—THIS VITAL piece of me otherwise known as my intuition, my inner voice, my heart, my wisdom. This was the grounding in myself that I'd been missing. I could still recall the feeling of handing myself over to the church men like a little girl giving something back to her disapproving father.

I thought back to my early days at the church. To those times when fear would overcome me and I'd freeze, not knowing what to say or how to respond. Times I didn't defend myself or get angry because women were supposed to be gentle-spirited. Then there were other times I felt I couldn't explain myself because feelings were primarily viewed as indications of sin and problems.

Life is a feeling experience. We experience life through our bodies. It accompanies every choice, decision, interaction, and moment of our lives. When a woman believes that her body is a problem or her feelings are wrong she will naturally try and separate from herself. She may spend years hating her body, shaming herself for the way she feels, or neglecting her needs. To separate from yourself is to stop knowing yourself, and to stop knowing yourself is to fall asleep to yourself.

Human beings are physical, emotional, and intellectual creatures. We are designed for whole-body intelligence. We have intuition. It is how a mother can sense her child is in danger from miles away. It is why we trust or mistrust a person we have just met even though we have no reason to. This knowing doesn't come from our head. It isn't found by intellectualizing or overthinking. It is some truth rooted deep within our gut, some truth our body is telling us. *This doesn't seem right. I need something. I do not feel good around this person. I don't want this. I do want this.*

I was right, I *did* know the truth about many things that felt wrong at the church. I just wasn't certain what it was that I knew. I couldn't name it and I discounted it. We need to understand that our bodies know things in advance of our conscious minds. It is not so important to know exactly why we feel something or understand a situation perfectly. The knowing comes first. The reason, the understanding, comes later. Our bodies are ahead of our minds. I repeat, our bodies are ahead of our minds.

The ways and wisdom of the feminine are generally considered less trustworthy in Western culture, so it makes sense that we would need to make some effort to reconnect with our inner guidance. This knowing isn't just part of who we are, it *is* who we are. Think of it like having an intelligent compass buried inside you that works only for you. It points you in a direction that is whole, courageous, and authentic for you and only you. Honoring this knowing isn't selfish, it is true and right.

My wisdom, my knowing, my intuition, my feelings, my inner guidance, my gut sense. Whatever we might call it, this was a precious thing I had been taught to discount. It explained the lack of confidence I had in myself while I was there: the lack of centeredness. I lost mine in the chaos and turmoil of trying to be someone else. And what hurt was that the church wanted it that way. They wanted to be my wisdom. At first I felt sick to realize that I had let this happen. But this was something I had the power to change.

As I began to acknowledge and trust my feelings again they swept in with an overwhelming rush. I felt my wires reconnecting. I sensed there was something greater and deeper and more vital happening. I was awakening to the truth and power I held within my own body. I was like the woman waking up after giving birth under twilight sleep. So many times the men had stood over me from their place in the pulpit telling me that my life of obedience and submission to their strict rules and suffocating laws was wonderful. But it wasn't wonderful. It was not wonderful at all.

• • •

To improve our lives and our health and to truly flourish, we must acknowledge the seamless unity between our beliefs, behaviors, and physical bodies.

Christiane Northrup, *Women's Bodies, Women's Wisdom*

freeing Eve.

THE DENIAL OF the feminine is planted firmly into the heart of Christianity, and a shocking amount of that denial is accomplished through the story of Eve.

Within the first few chapters of Genesis, Eve's wisdom, personhood, and dignity are called into question or negated altogether. Meanwhile, man's dominance, superior intelligence, and superior purpose over woman is established. It's awfully convenient for men who think very highly of themselves to have a God who also thinks this of them. We have a woman who has just been created by God and declared a thing of goodness and beauty and in the very next breath she is awful and wrong. She was beautiful. Then she was awful. The man was beautiful, too. And now, by comparison, he is extra beautiful. Praise God.

It seems impossible that this rhetoric is still effective in the twenty-first century, and yet it is. Every day pastors and leaders, men and women, stand in the pulpit and insist on an interpretation of Scripture that offers men a place of dominance over women, when they could just as easily insist on an interpretation that supports equality and respect for all people. But some don't. Some actively choose the denial of women while assuring them how wonderful it is.

Here is Eve. She is naked and lovely, and no one is bothered by this at first. It's a sunny, warm day, and she's sauntering through the lush garden when suddenly she sees this thing that she wants. We are told it is the fruit of a particular tree and that it is forbidden. We don't know what kind of fruit it is or exactly why it was forbidden. We just know she can't have it because *God said so.*

What was it, this thing that Eve was not supposed to take a bite of? What color was the flesh, and was it juicy? Was it dripping with deliciousness? And why wasn't the fruit given a name? Just about everything else in the story has a name. The man was called Adam. The woman was called Eve. The garden was named the garden of Eden. The tree was named the tree of the knowledge of good and evil. But the fruit? No name. Mystery fruit. Blank. X-variable. That seems to me to be a convenient omission. This makes the fruit a magical, mutating fruit. A blank slate. An ace to play. This makes it possible for the forbidden fruit to be whatever someone in authority wants it to be.

Eve's judgment comes down just as soon as she has taken a bite of her fruit. She has not even finished it! It's almost as if her hand is still dripping with the succulent juices when she is caught—literally red-handed—in her moment of delight. And even then she hadn't tried to keep it all for herself. As soon as she realized what a glorious thing she'd found she went to share it with the one person on earth she had to share it with! Meanwhile, someone is bothered by her nakedness, so she must cover up with a leaf.

I see a woman who has been misrepresented and punished unjustly to be used as an example. I see a brave woman who took initiative and was punished severely for it. A woman whose wisdom is discounted in order to make another's appear superior. I see a woman who is comfortable in her body and grounded there on earth. I see a woman who is relational and giving. Most of all, I see a woman punished for her curiosity.

Since Eve is not here to tell her own story we go on trust that the theologians have it right and have our best interests in mind. But what if they don't? What if Eve did exactly right by taking the fruit? What if she was supposed to have wisdom? What if she didn't need to cover up all her girly parts with a fig leaf because someone was afraid of her?

Because do you realize what that would mean? That would mean that we, the daughters of Eve, could have *everything* in the garden. As in every drippy, delicious, running-down-our-arms X-variable, no-name, blank thing that we want.

Eve's story is not our story. Eve's story is a story church men have told about a woman they have never met. She is the only one who can accurately tell her story, just as we are the only ones who can tell ours. If women are to be free from the heavy hand of patriarchy, we all must be free, and this includes Eve, who has been bound to a story that has in turn been bound to us. But if we free Eve from the false narrative that clings to her, we can free ourselves from our own.

finding anger.

AT MY MOTHER'S house I saw a thick black book on the shelf called *Women Who Run with the Wolves: Myths and Stories of the Wild Woman Archetype*. I pulled it down. The words on the cover stirred something in me. *Women. Wild. Wolves.* My mind flashed to a scene with me in the wild. *I am somewhere out in a vast plain with cliffs and caves and the occasional tree. My hair is knotty and crazy and I am barefoot and dirty, but my body is lean and taut from running and hunting. I am awake and alert, and I am carrying a spear. I can predict the weather by the hairs on my skin.*

I took the book, and I kept it by my bedside at night and carried it around with me during the day, hoping whatever was inside it would rub off on me. I almost didn't need to read it. I instinctively knew *Wild* was exactly what I needed. I'd had more than I could take of civilized. I was overcivilized. I was so civilized I was artificial. I couldn't feel my limbs or hear my own heartbeat.

Once it dawned on me the extent to which the church had sought to undermine my personhood and disrespect my body, I was angry, and that anger was a necessary, good thing. I had stifled that anger far too long already. To my surprise when I found anger I also found my will. Ah, that made perfect sense! Of course they work together! If they can get a woman to believe her anger is not valid, everything stays *fine.*

They turned me into a dog. Loyal, warm, wagging, trusting. And they led me right into a cage where they handed me a bone to chew and hoped I'd be satisfied enough to keep quiet. They did not even bother to give me the necessities and pleasures they so easily gave themselves. They told me it was for my own good.

No wonder I felt numb and lifeless. I'd been in that cage for too long. I hadn't done anything, touched anything, felt anything. My muscles were weak from underuse. I was covered in cloaks. I wanted to shed them all and run barefoot. I needed to feel my feet on the ground and feel life through my own skin. Get out of my head and forget what they said. I needed to be wild.

I used to be wild.

There are many living in these cages. I know because I see them claw and nip and fight. I watch them stand guard and protect what little they have for themselves. I see them attack in jealousy when another woman gets a larger piece. And I know what it is to be held down by a woman who doesn't want to share what she little has. And this is what I know.

Only starving women do that.

here and now.

UP UNTIL NOW, not going to church was unthinkable. Everybody knows if you stop going to church it's the same thing as slipping down a slide that is going to dump you out directly into the pit of hell, out of which you will never, ever be able to climb. It's not like those gymnastics pits with the foam cubes, which are also a desperate situation, but not nearly as permanent as hell, so you really need to count the cost. I had been weighing the cost for a while.

At this particular moment our family had been attending a small Baptist church led by a lovely couple with whom I had made a friendship. But then Josh decided to stop going to church altogether and the kids stopped along with him. I felt I should stick it out longer because the good woman doesn't die easily. But the truth was that church was making me ill. Even the loveliest church in the world couldn't make up for the fact that I had had too much church. My body was rejecting Bible verses with the strength of a bad case of food poisoning.

Still, the good woman made her case. So I tried going alone, but I'd just show up and cry, and it was getting difficult keeping my drippy nose and tears from dropping into the shared communion goblet. The real me begged for a break and argued her case back to the good woman. We decided on a compromise. I would take a break for one month and then we would reevaluate.

The next Sunday was heaven on earth. My family had gone hiking and the house was quiet. I woke up slow and easy, padded around in my pajamas, and thought about how wonderful it felt to let go of the belief that it is always right to press through suffering. I walked up to the bakery, bought a croissant and coffee, and brought it back to my kitchen to enjoy it. I looked up and around toward the ceiling. *Are you here too, God?* I laughed. Of course God was out here too.

The next morning I woke up, and it turned out that I had not slipped into the pit of hell. I was still in my bedroom. Over the next few weeks I experienced a tangible sense of healing in my soul and spirit and I realized just how much wisdom my body was holding for me. I felt lighter than I had in years. It was empowering to be taking care of me. Our feelings and our deepest longings are smart. They *are* leading us someplace. They know where we have come from, where we are presently, and where we are headed.

I could feel that I was on the right track, so I kept going. I got reacquainted with acceptance for myself and my feelings. I quieted other voices outside me and those in my head. I consulted myself more on decisions. I learned to listen. To slow down and pay attention.

As I did this a remarkable thing happened. I believed myself. I realized I'd been rewriting my feelings to make them fit my reality. A skill I'd learned entirely in church. I saw also that my reality had been narrated to me by others, including my husband. And I had been seeing things how I thought they should be, not how they actually were. My perception shifted. I looked around at my life. I looked at myself, my husband, and my children through this new lens. That's when my life finally started to make sense.

• • •

> *When we acknowledge our needs, listen to the dictates of our souls, and release the emotional pain that results from denial, we are put immediately in touch with our hearts, our feelings, and our inner guidance system. Our intellects and thoughts can now assume their rightful role: being of service to our hearts and our deepest knowing, not the other way around.*
>
> Christiane Northrup, *Women's Bodies, Women's Wisdom*

seeing me.

I WAS ON my bed in lingerie holding huge blossoms of white hydrangeas I'd cut from the garden. At the end of my bed a selfie stick was perched on top a stack of books that sat on top of a kitchen stool. I was taking the first undressed photos of myself I had ever taken in my life. I purchased a camera app, and in no time at all I had fifty photos. I leaned back on my pillow to scroll through them.

Awkward. Delete.

Trying too hard. Delete.

Side angle is nice. Save.

Pretty pose. Save.

I was taking an online class about healing the way you see yourself. I told no one I was doing this. I wasn't sure about it going in, but it was for women healing from body and sexual shame, and it sounded like just what I needed. I had to admit after all those years of buttoning up my blouse to the tippity-top button, it was surprisingly freeing to be naked. And a bit awkward too. I'd grown less connected, less comfortable with my body and my sexuality in the church.

Being a woman is complicated. Why do we ask women to hide so much of their beauty? We love it and we want to see it. But if we show it, we are shamed for it. Impossible. We are cast as bad or good depending how we look, how we dress. People want to see us and then they want to hide us. We are adored, worshipped, praised, or scorned depending on the context or who might see. So many mixed messages.

But I was remembering now. My body was good. Every inch of my body was good. And it was mine.

Reconnecting to my sexuality was so important to my health and happiness and wholeness. I could see now that the church had been uncomfortable with pleasure. With delight. With sex. With women. But that didn't mean that I had to be.

I put the flowers down and changed into black lingerie. I set my camera back up on the books and got ready for another round. I knew what I had to do. I had to kill the good woman. She was my worst enemy. She had wrapped herself around me like a mummy, suffocating me for years, and I hated her. *I don't want to be her anymore.*

• • •

In finding our own story, we assemble all the parts of ourselves.

Marion Woodman, *Leaving My Father's House*

honesty.

I THOUGHT BACK to my wedding night and to my honeymoon. I remembered the guy from the woodshed. I thought about how my husband and I stopped kissing almost as soon as we were married and how I hadn't really noticed. I thought about how he never came up behind me while I was washing the dishes or put his hands around my waist like Steve Martin does to Diane Keaton in *Father of the Bride*. I thought about how I hadn't exactly welcomed his touch. And I finally acknowledged what I hadn't ever felt free to acknowledge. I did not really like having sex with my husband.

The fact of the matter is my body had never been properly invited to our religion. Not beyond being a functional piece of machinery anyway. What my body could provide for others was the first order of business. Producing children. Pleasure for the husband. Meals. A clean house. Volunteer service. Women had not been encouraged to experience their own presence, let alone their sexuality.

It's not that I didn't enjoy it ever. That wasn't quite it. It was that we didn't move toward each other in that way naturally. I had not welcomed his advances. I knew I had never given myself to him completely in that way. That was something I had never been able to pretend.

And I had always wanted to feel beautiful to my husband. I think that is a legitimate thing to want. But I am not sure he found me any more beautiful than I found him desirable. I do remember catching his glance once. It was the summer we rented a house on Anna Maria Island, the year after our first child was born. I had a new bathing suit that year. Lavender, with a halter top—it was a great color on me. I saw him do a double take, and he said my eyes looked really blue. I felt pretty to him that day. But do you know, in nineteen years of marriage my husband never once looked into my eyes and told me I was beautiful.

• • •

> *The body recognizes the conscious truth of the relationship before the psyche does.*
>
> Marion Woodman, *Leaving My Father's House*

fragile.

I MULLED ON these past memories from my bed, staring at my four beige walls and out the one small window, where all I could see was the weather and the greenish-brown wood shingles of the house next door. It was raining again.

My collection of pieces of me was growing larger. I found my dreams, my identity, my voice, my knowing. I reclaimed my feelings, my body, and my sexuality. Every day I felt more whole. But it sounded exhausting to start over. So much time had been lost. Years I could have been developing myself, growing, thriving. But the magnitude of this latest revelation—the lost intimacy in my marriage was almost more than I could bear. It was easier to roll over and sleep.

Just outside my door I heard my family in the living room laughing together. My heart sank. I wanted to be out there too, but I didn't belong to that family out there anymore. Not in the same way. I couldn't stand the way I could see truth now. Too much truth. If I stayed in my bedroom, maybe I wouldn't have to feel it.

When would I be free from this story? I wanted out. I wanted a do-over. I wanted to have listened to my mother. To have trusted my gut more. To have been braver.

I looked at the hook on the back of the door, and I imagined what I would use to tie myself up there and wondering if it would hold. I didn't have any rope. Maybe a scarf. The silk pink one from Turkey might work.

Occasionally one of the kids would knock on the door and peek their head in to check on me. If they came in at all, they came in gingerly. I could tell they saw me as fragile. I was fragile.

change or die.

AT THE AIRPORT I bought a book by Sally Fields to distract me on the trip. I felt guilty for spending the money. Airport books were so overpriced. I got my phone out to text Josh to ask if he minded, and then I stopped myself. *Don't ask for permission, just buy the damn book.*

We were going to Kentucky to spend the weekend with Rich, the counselor who had helped us so effectively when we were struggling in ministry. This time we would spend the entire weekend with him and his wife.

Josh and I didn't sit together on the plane, and the Sally Fields book didn't hold my attention. Instead of reading I just sat there with my tray table down thinking about what we were about to do. Decide the fate of our marriage. If we did let it go, this would absolutely be the end of the good woman—if there were any shreds of her left. The church would condemn me. Not that long ago that sounded unbearable, but now it just sounded—irrelevant.

I didn't know whether I wanted this marriage or not anymore. I did not want to end it, but I did not want to be in it either. Thriving was a requirement for my life moving forward, and sadly, I could no longer ignore the fact that I had never truly thrived in my marriage. Still, I never wanted to have to bring my children into the living room to tell them that their family was ending. And to that end I clung until there was nothing left to cling to.

We landed, and as soon as I stepped off the plane the warm, thick air hit me at once. My insides were anxious, but I had no doubt we were in good hands with Rich. He would get us through this. One way or another, it was time to change or die.

Part Seven

BRAVER THINGS

sharing our stories.

I STUMBLED THROUGH the end of my marriage just as I stumbled through the beginning. Perhaps if circumstances had been different, we could have managed to make it work. But they weren't and we couldn't. Love comes in many forms and sometimes it looks like letting go.

Once I was outside my relationship, it was much easier to see why it had been unhealthy for me. It's hard to see relationships, families, churches clearly when you are in the middle of them. Any system that enables men to hold authority over women, and husbands over wives, is unreasonable and outdated. This practice robs a woman of her full personhood. Her right to self-ownership and self-government are at best undermined. The fullness of her identity is denied. And the potential for her further suffering is compounded by a culture that glorifies suffering.

What makes this view especially misleading in some churches is that the potential for harm is hidden. And before any talk of breaking free from this system can take place, a woman has to see it as hurtful in the first place. I know many women find it fulfilling to devote themselves to the man they love. I did. And I know that some marriages are genuinely healthy—both partners are getting what they need because, thankfully, love and respect are at the foundation of the relationship. If my marriage had been able to support my aspirations or hadn't been complicated by church bias, bigotry, and sexism, it is possible that I might have never seen a problem.

But I am aware now. This experience has opened my eyes to the oppression that others have faced. It has given me compassion I didn't have before. It has helped me see the connections between power, politics, and religion.

I understand now that the men who made these rules were white, privileged men who have never put their own lives on hold indefinitely. They ask something of women they have never asked of themselves and can never fully comprehend. And whether it was out of ignorance or deliberate, they misrepresented the truth of what submission really means for the women in their churches.

Will they listen to my story? It is unlikely. It is more likely they will caution women not to listen to it. They might say I am embittered or discredit me as someone not worthy to speak. They might suggest that my limited theological academic credentials make my story less valuable, attack my character, or use my own words and phrases against me. They might reframe my story and my experience in a way that protects their illusions. But most of all they will try not to hear it because they are afraid of what it might cost them if they do. And because of that fear, young women who might benefit from my story won't get to hear it. And they will have their bodies shamed and their dreams shattered and their eyes and ears covered and their mouths muzzled, and they will fall asleep all over again until they wake up and tell their stories.

the giving tree.

IN *The Giving Tree* a little boy became friends with a tree. He would climb up her trunk, swing from her branches, and devour her apples, and the story tells us, "The tree was happy." The boy went away and forgot about the tree, but came back later as a young man and asked the tree for money. The tree had no money, but she gave him her apples so he could sell them, and the story tells us, "The tree was happy." The boy went away again and came back years later, this time wanting a home and a wife. The tree could not give him a home or a wife, but she gave him her branches so he could build a home, and the story tells us, "The tree was happy." The boy went away again for a long time, and when he finally returned he asked for a boat. The tree had no boat, but she gave him her trunk so he could make a canoe, and then the story tells us, "The tree was happy. But not really." The boy went away one last time for a long, long time, and when he returned he was a very old man. The tree was sorry she had nothing left to give him since now she was just an old stump. But the old man said he was tired now and "stumps are good for resting," so he sat down on her. And the story ends.

This story always felt a bit confusing to me as a child. Was it a story about a generous tree? Or was it about a selfish boy? Or was the story about a tree who gave too much?

Well, here is my version of the story.

Once there was a young woman who became friends with a church. The church leaders said to the young woman, "Can we have your past? Give us your old life, let us take it so we can make you new, because that will 'make God happy.'" So the woman gave up her old life so God would be happy. Then the church leaders said, "Can we have your money? We need it to pay our pastors and keep our programs running because that will 'make God happy.'" So the woman gave her money to the church so God would be happy. Then the church leaders said to the woman, "Can we have your talents? We are making a new music label and if you sing only for us and no one else that will 'make God happy.'" So the woman gave her singing to the church so God would be happy. Then the church leaders said, "Give us your children, because we will need their devotion and money and talents one day and that will 'make God happy.'" So the woman started to give up her children, but then she realized the church leaders were greedy and would take from her children the same things they had taken from her and she could not let that happen. So she left.

• • •

For me it has been a lesson in boundaries. Each of us alone must advocate for our own health, happiness, and well-being. But that is especially difficult to do when the lines between the powerful and the vulnerable are blurry or erased altogether. Then, like the giving tree, we may end up giving so much of ourselves that we nearly self-destruct. Perhaps that is because we don't know our own value.

The hierarchy in the church is built on the principle that a woman's wisdom is broken. So when a young woman walks through the church doors, before she has even found a seat, her value as a person has been weakened and an important boundary line has already been crossed. This is why reestablishing our value and trust in ourselves, and redrawing the lines of where we begin and end as a person are some of the most self-defining tasks we can do. When our emotional, physical, intellectual, and spiritual boundaries are intact we are less vulnerable to those who might take advantage of our abundant, desirable resources.

Self-preservation isn't selfish, it's smart. All living things do the work of self-preservation. Nature shows us the ways of protection, rhythm, and balance. A tree has a thick layer of bark. A turtle has a shell. A bee has a sting. A woman's life is a balancing act, no doubt. And there are times when immense giving is inevitable. But we should never give our souls away, not even to our children. All throughout our lives we need to stay connected to ourselves at the core.

The church attempted to care about my connection to myself but was unfortunately mistaken about what true connection involves. For instance, as a young wife and mother, I was encouraged to take time away from my normal routine to have time alone. On the surface it sounded generous. Sometimes I would go to a coffee shop to read or think or journal. It was nice to get time away, but ultimately what it gave me was a false sense of connection with myself, since the theology I was beholden to did not allow me to assess my own well-being, happiness, relationships, or purpose. The most I could do was spend this time recommitting myself to do more of the things I was already doing.

Eventually, this shallow connection revealed itself for what it was. It showed up in my life as chronic anxiety and a frenetic pace. It showed up as me playing the martyr or complaining. It showed up as hurt and depression or withdrawal and silence. These were all signs that care was needed. But the church's answer to many of these kinds of problems was a pat on the head and a verse about the boundary lines having fallen in pleasant places, and I was not empowered to make change for myself.

Humans are not meant to live like this—in constant dissociation and denial, smothering and silencing the messages of our bodies and our spirits. This can actually lead to sickness, disease, and even death. I wonder, what would the giving tree have been like if she'd been an empowered tree?

The empowered tree stands strong and grounded. She feels her roots running deep underground and cool water running through her veins. The sunshine and birds frolic on her branches. In her seasons she provides shade, beauty, nuts, and fruit. And when the boy asks for all her branches to make a house, she knows he does not see her greater value. "Sorry, boy," she says, smiling, "you'll have to find another way." She is green and vibrant and healthy and happy. And when no one is looking she magically turns sunlight into food and oxygen. She is doing all that she was created to do.

the bravest thing.

FRED ROGERS SAID, "Love is the root of everything—all learning, all parenting, all relationships. Love, or the lack of it." When I was younger, I thought throwing all of life under the umbrella of a little word like *love* seemed too simplistic. But the older I get the more I realize that it is the simple things in life that are most difficult to do well. The word *love* may be simple, but loving is not.

I assumed the church understood love. I assumed it loved me, a woman. It never occurred to me that misogyny was a reason behind the teaching of submission. Or that shaming those living outside the box of patriarchal norms was really just a way of hiding hatred and fear. This has to be one of the greatest ironies of the church. To proclaim a Creator so loudly, yet disrespect the creation so deeply.

It is my observation that fear and love won't share the same space. Whichever force is stronger will push the other out. When fear is in charge, love doesn't stand a chance. Fear gets in the way of love because it hinders relationship, and love is built on relationship. Instead, fear drives the need for control. Fear causes us to keep our distance from those who are "different" or "unusual" or "nontraditional." Fear of the unknown makes us cling ever so tightly to what has always been. The familiar feels right to us simply because it is what we already know. But relationship is the path to love. It is when we sit down with someone and share food, laughter, or something of our story, that a relationship begins. Now love can grow from that.

The institutional church must decide what their mandate is. If it is simply to make converts or fix those they believe to be broken, then perhaps they'll continue on with it brutally, as they have many times throughout history. But if the mandate is to love? Then they must first deal with their fear.

Jesus demonstrated the connection between love and relationship throughout his ministry. He talked and ate with those that others shunned. He spent time with and touched those called unclean. He despised superiority and finger pointing. He often chose to build relationship, break down barriers, remove shame, and restore dignity. And he was harshly criticized for doing these things. Why? Because love isn't simple. It is brave.

• • •

There is no fear in love. But perfect love drives out fear.
1 John 4:18 NIV

something less than love.

IN THE END, the church's definition of love did not match my experience. The church, my husband, and me. We were a triangle. Three entities with three different definitions of love, three different experiences of love, and three different goals for love.

The church was primarily concerned with securing commitment to its hierarchal structures. Roles and rules came first. Love came second. I wanted acceptance, respect, intimacy, genuine knowing, seeing, and sharing. I wanted the chance to reach my full potential. I thought I would get these things when I married. I thought our relationship would grow and change as we grew and changed as people, but that did not happen. Instead, I committed to a specific, fixed role that was not to ever change.

I did not understand that in my husband's mind marrying a woman was something like checking a box on a to-do list. Wife, check. Mother, check. I do not think he fully understood he was marrying a woman with needs of her own. But this is what he was taught in his family and his church. The church says, "If you have marriage, you have love and intimacy." But that was not true for our relationship. Yes, we loved one another, but we could not sustain our relationship based on the teachings of the church alone. I did not always want to go where my husband was leading. And there was not enough room in our marriage for me.

Marriage is not a guarantee of love and intimacy. Marriage is the "house" or the container where a relationship lives. The house is just the outer structure. The house tells you nothing about the relationship inside it. It does not tell you anything about the quality or depth of the love that resides inside. Some will find love inside their marriage house. But others may find something less. Still others may find something worse.

It is not the church's job to define the words that make up the meaning of our lives. What it means for me to be a woman is up to me. What I will or won't accept as love is, too. It is not enough to call something love. I need love to feel like love.

permission.

I HAVE SPENT the majority of this book talking about how I came to know my truth. How I came to hear my own voice and distinguish it from all the other voices I was hearing. And how I came to believe in its value. Believing yourself is part of it. The other part is figuring out what to do.

We had an extraordinary theater director at the church, and one year she asked me to help with the music for a show she was directing. It was *Joseph and the Amazing Technicolor Dreamcoat*. It had been a handful of years since I had done much besides cooking, cleaning, schooling, and hosting, so I jumped at the opportunity. Rehearsals were spread out over the course of the whole year, which meant I had something to look forward to every week. While I was doing this I realized that my dream still hadn't died. I knew that if it was still there after all these years, I had to do something about it.

I approached the director and asked if she would talk with me. We'd connected over theater early on and I had admired her through the years. Her father had been the head of the drama department at a major university. I thought if anyone in the church could understand me, she could. It was a big deal for me to open up to her. I hadn't dreamed of possibilities for myself in years.

I will never forget that conversation, because as we strolled around the parking lot that afternoon I did not get the answer I wanted. As I shared with her my desire to pursue a career in musical theater, I felt the same disconnect between my words and her words that I'd felt in my conversations with my husband. It was as if no one could hear what I was saying. For instance, if you said, "I am thirsty and I need water," and the person replied, "Look how pretty that tree is!" Tears began streaming down my face and turned into sobbing in my despair. I see now that I was looking for permission. But no one seemed able to envision a different reality for me than what it was already. Nobody could show me a bridge from where I was standing to where I wanted to go.

I was desperate for some fairy godmother to come and tap me with her wand and say it was okay. But she never came. No one could rescue me but me. Things only changed when I learned to give myself permission.

There are often risks and losses at stake when we decide to take responsibility for ourselves. Marriages, jobs, children, relationships with your community, or family opinions hang in the balance. Living out your truth can wreak major havoc on life as you now know it. This is not a neat and tidy business we are talking about. This is a soul-searching, gut-wrenching, tear-jerking business, and only you can decide whether what you are facing is something you can live with or demands change. Yes, it can be messy, but messy can be good.

Some of you still don't think that you can ask the world to change for you or accommodate you. Let me assure you the universe is big enough to hold you. If your world crumbles because you have started to value or believe yourself, then let it, because it means that you were the only one holding it up. Let it go. It is the only way a more supportive universe can emerge in its place.

Remember, there is a world of difference between living life *for yourself* and living life *as yourself* in a way that is meaningful and aligned with who you are or who you want to be. One has to do with thinking about yourself and the other has to do with honoring yourself. Living as your authentic self *is* giving, by the way. The real, authentic you is literally the best thing you have to give to anybody. When you do that you won't just be living, you'll be radiating.

Maybe you won't feel ready to act or maybe it's not even possible right now. You can still begin a new relationship with yourself. You can change it from being one of denial, performance, and judgment to one of love, acceptance, and authenticity. You don't actually have to go anywhere to come home to yourself.

One thing I have learned is that sometimes we have more power in a situation than we think we do, but we just can't see it. The next time you find yourself in a situation where you feel stuck or powerless, look around and see if you can find where you have power to make change. Notice where your feelings don't match up with your actions. Or, where your values don't match up with your reality. You are the bridge to what you want. You are the only one who can change the story.

You don't need permission from anyone outside of you, but for some reason it helps to hear it. So I am here to tell you. You have permission! You have the right to own yourself and your life. You have permission to reimagine your present, future, and yes, even your past. You have the right to reclaim your all your missing pieces. The question is, what do you want?

courage.

I THINK THAT is what the church never wanted—for me to wake up and realize it wasn't more obedience that I needed. It was more courage. We were taught we did not belong to ourselves; I needed courage to do just that. We were taught to live for the church's values; I needed courage to live by my own. We were taught to become the women they imagined; I needed courage to become the woman I imagined.

A few years ago I met a woman named Joanna. Joanna left conservative Christianity and was now living in LA with her husband and working as a playwright. As I got to know her I couldn't believe how similar our experiences were as young women in the church. Joanna had also gotten heavily involved in a ministry, gotten married in the church, and had a female mentor who delivered to her the same "death of a dream" speech that my mentor had given me. This woman had given up her dream of becoming a PE teacher, and she felt it only right that Joanna should give up her dream of becoming a playwright.

Like me, Joanna let her dreams die until she eventually came to the same conclusion I did. Dreams matter. They matter a lot. And if no one in the church was going to give her permission to have them, she would just have to give permission to herself. All this dream killing really is a lack of imagination. It is a sure and steady death to live among people who have no imagination for you. It's not a place you want to stay for long.

Women disempower each other when they have not been empowered. That is because we cannot give something we do not have. But once we learn to give ourselves permission we will naturally give it to each other because we will already have done it for ourselves.

wholeness.

IT MIGHT SOUND pessimistic, but I think most of us will have some time in our lives when we realize the fairy tale isn't real and our hopes are dashed to bits. We don't talk about these things enough in our kitchens and neighborhoods and churches. What happens after the wedding. The loss of a child. The realities of marriage. Addictions, abuse, betrayals inside our own families. Things we discovered about ourselves later. People we shouldn't have trusted. Investments that ran amok. No matter how hard we try to hold things together, sometimes they still fall apart.

Leaving behind the church's expectations for me was harder than I thought it would be. Those expectations were so ingrained in me they had become my own. But I couldn't be the good woman and also be true to myself or whole. I couldn't keep abandoning my dreams, dismissing legitimate feelings or pretending away truth. I needed to live in integrity with myself. But first I had to let some illusions crumble.

The church of all places should be a refuge where it is safe to be human. And yet I found it was the church that struggled to associate with the not-so-pretty things—the suffering, the weak, the broken. They so wish to avoid being identified with the appearance of failure. Leaders scoot away from the fallen as fast as they can manage. *He must not have been one of us*, they say. The dividing wall goes up; the finger of shame is pointed. The church's opportunity to love and remember its own humanity is lost. It is disappointing. Because until the church is willing to go to hellish places with people who are hurting they will continue to live lives steeped in illusion, disconnected from reality.

It's a love problem. To accept imperfection in ourselves and in each other we have to feel safe that we will be loved for who we are and not for our performance. But deep down we know that we aren't. Most of the time we would rather pretend than face feeling unloved.

I realize there are people who believe that I have failed and failed my children, and I'm okay with that. I wasn't always, though. Having my life fall apart publicly has shown me the worst that can happen, and do you know what it is? People criticize you. That is about it. And when they are finished criticizing you they go to Home Depot and buy a new grill because they are on sale. In the old value system, I simply could not have my marriage end and still be the good woman. But she isn't real and I am. I don't want to live my life for an ideal or in fear of judgment anymore. I need to be driven by what is in my heart. To hold onto something we know is no longer true is its own sort of madness.

I don't think I failed my marriage. I think my marriage failed me. But even if I had failed my marriage, that still wouldn't make me a failure. That would make me a human. I have owned my choices and learned from them, and I am not deterred. I have forgiven myself for failing to be perfect. And I forgive the church for failing to be perfect, too.

There is a lot more to a person than the good woman or the bad woman. A real, whole life is lived in the space between perfection and failure. There is "both-and" in addition to "either-or." There are choices in addition to laws. There is process in addition to product. There is the "here and now" in addition to "someday." There is being in addition to performing. There is compassion instead of judgment. Striving for the impossible—perfection—pulls us out of life. Wholeness is a kinder goal. It grounds us in love and reality because it demands that we ask ourselves what our real and present needs are.

> *Perfection belongs to the gods: completeness or wholeness is the most a human being can hope for.*
>
> Marion Woodman, *Addiction to Perfection*

thriving.

THE FIRST THING I do every morning after I wake up is fill up my blue and white electric kettle, feed my cat, put three and a half scoops of coffee into my French press, and take my antidepressant. I say this proudly, by the way. My antidepressant reminds me that I've been through a lot, yes, but it is also a reminder that I don't have to try to heal all by myself.

Glenda was the third counselor I tried. It took a while to find the right person. The first woman I tried was clearly on some power trip. I spent the majority of our first session filling out a form while she stared me down impersonally from her chair three feet across from me in her sparse, unwelcoming room. I left feeling worse than when I came. The second woman I tried didn't think the church had anything to do with my problems.

It took Glenda only one hour to have my life figured out. And to inform me that I'd lived with anxiety at the church for so long I thought it was normal. She's been one of the beautiful people who have helped me find my footing again. She's shared a number of helpful resources with me, but I wanted to share one that was especially helpful called the Personal Bill of Rights. If your value as a human being has been diminished, it is likely your rights have been too. This list can help you assert your needs and create healthier boundaries for yourself. Glenda read them aloud to me, and it was powerful to hear them that way. Consider having someone read them to you.

Personal Bill of Rights

1. I have the right to ask for what I want.
2. I have the right to say no to requests or demands I can't meet.
3. I have the right to express all of my feelings, positive or negative.
4. I have the right to change my mind.
5. I have the right to make mistakes and not have to be perfect.
6. I have the right to follow my own values and standards.
7. I have the right to say no to anything when I feel I am not ready, it is unsafe, or it violates my values.
8. I have the right to determine my own priorities.
9. I have the right *not* to be responsible for others' behavior, actions, feelings, or problems.
10. I have the right to expect honesty from others.
11. I have the right to be angry at someone I love.
12. I have the right to be uniquely myself.
13. I have the right to feel scared and say, "I'm afraid."
14. I have the right to say, "I don't know."
15. I have the right not to give excuses or reasons for my behavior.
16. I have the right to make decisions based on my feelings.
17. I have the right to my own needs for personal space and time.
18. I have the right to be playful and frivolous.
19. I have the right to be healthier than those around me.
20. I have the right to be in a nonabusive environment.
21. I have the right to make friends and be comfortable around people.
22. I have the right to change and grow.
23. I have the right to have my needs and wants respected by others.

24. I have the right to be treated with dignity and respect.
25. I have the right to be happy.

My mantra for healing became, "Does this contribute to my thriving?" *Thriving* became my word to live by. I like it because it feels very neutral. It has no past history for me. Language is a powerful tool for better or for worse and I am convinced that it is one of the church's most powerful weapons of mass destruction. It is why using our own words is an important step in taking ownership of our experience. Otherwise, we get caught in a language trap where our experiences can remain unvalidated. Stepping outside the church's "approved" vocabulary allows us to put our experiences into our own words so we can understand and communicate our truth without apology.

love to me then.

"YOUR CHILDREN NEED to know they were born in love," the counselor said.

I wasn't prepared for that comment. It hadn't occurred to me that in my desire to take a thick, black Sharpie pen and smear over the papers of the last twenty years of my life, I might undermine my children's sense of history—their connection to their dad and me and their happy family memories. I was so absorbed in my own life that I had forgotten that this was their story, too.

My eyes started to tear because that was just it. I wasn't sure I believed that. Were they born in love? How can I believe that was love? Then the counselor said something that I will never forget. He said that I could believe my children were born in love because at the time it was my best consciousness of love. He said it was love to me *then.*

I thought about that for a second.

Okay. I can believe that. I will try to believe that.

It was love to me then.

what our children need.

WHEN MY CHILDREN were young, it was easier to buy into the idea that I was their authority. No, they could not jump into the pool until I was ready and yes, they absolutely did have to take a nap and eat their vegetables. They needed me to not let them put their teeny-tiny finger in a light socket or pet the ferocious-looking dog. There was no way around the fact that I was their authority.

But as my children grew older I began to notice that my faith and my philosophy of parenting were not always in agreement with each other. My faith asked me to ensure that my children grew up obedient to my authority. My faith asked me to ensure that my children adopted the same religious beliefs I had at the time. In other words, I had the goods and I needed to get them to take it. In my role as my children's teacher I was working from an entirely different position. I was trying to offer them a broad education and an environment that was nurturing, flexible, and open. I wanted my children to think for themselves, ask questions, and stay curious. I wasn't attempting to be the one holding all the information (I wasn't) whose job was to stuff their heads full of all that I knew. In that role I saw myself as a facilitator, not an authority.

According to the church, I was supposed to be creating children. According to my philosophy of teaching, I was discovering them. It was an impossible task the church asked of me. I am a woman, not a factory. And obedience is a life skill, not a life purpose. My children deserved the chance to explore the world and come to their own conclusions about life and God just as I had been free to do. Just as we all eventually do.

We often charge children with the duty to respect authority. But what about our duty as adults to respect the child? Again, it goes back to respecting the personhood of another individual. Are we creating a specific person out of this child we have? Or are we nurturing a whole human being?

When we are living our own lives to uphold an illusion of perfection, then we need our children to contribute to that illusion. But when we let go of perfection—when we pop that balloon and let the air out of it—we can all exhale. Parents exhale. Children exhale. Our whole lives relax and we can just be.

Children are not easily fooled. They know there is more to life than obedience and plastic appearances. They may not have names for all their experiences yet, but they are excellent truth seers. They see through our façades, whatever yours or mine may be. Children need parents brave enough to be authentic. Let them see the real you, not the you you think you should be. Let them live in the real world with you, not the world you think it should be. And please don't tell your children they have terrible, evil hearts unless you want to be remembered as the one who crushed their beautiful soul. Whatever you do, don't let that be you.

light God, kind God.

WHEN ALL IS said and done the spiritual journey is still one we each take alone. It is the thoughts we have when no one else is around. It is what we believe or don't believe and what that means to us. Our spiritual life is private and personal to us. On the other hand, religion is shared with a larger community. Religion can offer a sense of connection and tangible support. It can be a place to find comfort, hope, and community. But religion should serve our spirits and not the other way around. Our spirits should never be slaves to our religion.

It is natural for humans to want to make sense of God. That, to me, is what religion ultimately is. Humanity's attempt to make sense of God. To capture God in a kind of capsule that can be replicated and shared. I don't know if God exists, but if so, then I have a feeling God is like music. Music comes to life by and through human expression. That is the beauty of it, the personalized nature of it. No two people hear or play the same piece of music in the exact same way. Whether we are the one writing or playing or listening, it isn't about doing it right. It is about taking it in, experiencing it and letting it mean something to our hearts.

God and religion are not the same thing. Religion carries with it great potential for good and for harm. It's humans that make it more complicated (and more certain) and heavier than it needs to be. Religion shouldn't be something heavy we give each other to carry. It would be better to have no religion than one that is a burden, or does more harm than good, or fails to respect and love all living creatures.

I mentioned earlier that my music professor said that I'd used restraint in my composition. He also said that in his years of experience, restraint was something he'd found difficult to teach. I had purposely kept the piece simple because I loved the melody and I wanted that to be the thing people remembered. Maybe there is something to this? Maybe sharing a beautiful religion isn't only about knowing what to include, but knowing what to leave out.

the old knowing.

I WANT TO go back to where my story began. You may remember I shared at the beginning of this book that my mother warned me not to trust the man at church. My mother, who had proven a thousand lifetimes over that she loves me and has my back. My mother, who spoke with fiery eyes and a commanding voice and told me not to trust the charmer. Still, I trusted the charmer. I took the shiny apple. Someone please tell me, how old is this story?

I entered the adult world both fortunate and naïve. I grew up riding my bike to the homes of teachers who fed me cookies. In summer, my neighborhood had a bookmobile that came by the pool during adult swim so all of us drippy kids could pick out a book. I was fortunate enough to grow up not knowing what a jungle this world is.

I started out my book talking about fear and how fear became my prison. I see now that the original source of this fear was not my own, but rather the church's fear projected onto me. They had their own reasons for being afraid, but also at work was an old, old fear that has been carried along toward women for thousands of years.

In her book *Women Who Run with the Wolves*, Dr. Clarissa Pinkola Estes talks about how women have been maligned, oppressed, and hunted in ways similar to wild animals like bears and wolves. She talks about how wolves and women have been cast as evil characters and pushed to the outskirts of community. And how for generations our stories have often been altered, snuffed out, and silenced. As a result, women have lost what she calls "the old knowing": ways of women that are connected to nature, to our bodies, to each other, and all of the earth. Freer and wilder ways of being we might understand today if Christian patriarchy had not come in determined to "clean up the lands."

Herein lies the healing. Those parts of ourselves that have been injured, the very targets of our disempowerment—I suspect these are where our greatest power, joy, and vitality are hidden. We need to restore our connection to our own wisdom, to nature and our bodies, to our own fulfillment in work and pleasure, and to our own ways of being and doing. Not just for us but for the good of humankind. The world is desperate for these missing pieces too. It is not a coincidence that mother nature is finding her voice at the same time women are finding theirs. She has been long-suffering, but now she says, "Enough." And like the monsoons and rising waters, women are rising too.

home.

I'M FORTY-EIGHT NOW. It's about 8 p.m., and I'm sitting at my glossy white city table that I love. I bought it to replace the rustic farm table that made me sad because all our family memories were mixed up with that table. I'm cooking salmon and a sweet potato, and I'm drinking a glass of inexpensive red wine and writing this book.

It has been seven years since I started unlearning many of the things I learned from church. I have done an astonishing amount of unlearning, undoing, and letting go. It feels as though I have shed a thousand coats. But I can see myself again. I am glad to put this intense season of introspection behind me. As life at church was unbalanced, so was the healing. But I feel I am at equilibrium again.

Growth is always painful, but on the other side the reward has proven to me that the well-being of *all* the individuals inside a family or community is essential. We cannot ignore each other's suffering, or dictate a solution for the lives of others. We are all connected and bound by nature and history. And I'm grateful I did not have to go through it alone. I've had the loving support of family, friends, and trusted advisors to help me and guide me.

My family has changed and grown by leaps and bounds. Josh lives just a few blocks away from my youngest and me. We bump into each other at the grocery store and stop to chat. Our oldest child has just graduated from university and started a job in design. I am thrilled she can provide for herself, which will give her freedom to make the choices that are best for her. Our middle child trusted his instincts and dropped out of college when the pandemic hit. He moved to New York City to work for a start-up that saw his potential, and I thought he was brave. Our youngest is sixteen. They love science and are thriving in their academics. I am so happy they are in a place where they can be true to themselves.

And me? I am not the woman I wanted to be. I am not the person I once was. But I am much more than that now. I have learned to know and trust myself. I have learned to love and accept myself. Would that have happened without the church? I don't know.

But I feel good. Not just tonight, but good in general. I don't have a man. I don't know precisely where I'm going. But I am making new dreams. And I am whole. And I am home.

THE END

ACKNOWLEDGMENTS

I WOULD LIKE to acknowledge the extraordinary people who helped to make this book:

To Lisa Kloskin, my wonderful editor, thank you for sharing my vision for this book from the very beginning. Thank you for giving me so much freedom to develop the material and as a writer, for your skilled and thoughtful editing, and for the innumerable ways and hours you spent making the book better, clearer, and more cohesive. You are a true collaborator.

To the team at Broadleaf Books, thank you for this amazing opportunity, and to everyone who offered their time, talents, and dedication to bring this book to print.

To Alexander Field and Ingrid Beck at the Bindery Agency, your enthusiasm several years ago spurred me on to write it in the first place. Ingrid Beck, my agent, without your essential contributions we wouldn't be here! Also, for reading drafts and your timely encouragements.

To Milt Hendrickson, my father, without you this book simply would not have been possible. You are the gentle giant in my life, quietly supporting me, always backstage. Know that any success I have or may have in life is very much because of you.

To Mitzi Ash, my mother, for making this book as much a part of your life as it was mine. From taking my daily (and sometimes multidaily) calls and helping me flesh out ideas, to rewriting paragraphs, to finding just the right word. You read and edited this book more times than I did. I never imagined we'd do this together and it was the best surprise gift ever.

To Dale Ash, for lending your writing and storytelling expertise on numerous occasions, for brainstorming at the outset, for revising key portions, and challenging me to be a better, clearer writer.

To James A. Beverley, PhD, for so generously lending your time and expertise in the field of religion to my book. Thank you for reading drafts and staying up late to meet my deadlines. Your friendship and encouragement have been an unexpected gift.

To Shelley Reinhart, you lived this story with me. Thank you for reading drafts, cheering me on, keeping me alive, and telling me the truth. You are an extraordinary woman and friend.

To Joanna Breault, for reading drafts and fielding panic attacks, but mostly for wanting to see this book succeed and for our wonderful friendship.

To Richard Plass, PhD, your care and counsel during a difficult season were unforgettable. I wish everyone could have you for a counselor.

To Nigel Cornwall, my neighbor, for your invaluable assistance with all things technological.

To Emma, JQ, and Lake, for embracing big changes with courage and resilience. You each inspire me!

A special thank you to these author companions: Dr. Clarissa Pinkola Estes (*Women Who Run with the Wolves*), Marion Woodman (*Leaving My Father's House, Conscious Femininity*), Dr. Christiane Northrup (*Women's Bodies, Women's Wisdom*), Glennon Doyle (*Untamed*), and Sue Monk Kidd (*The Dance of the Dissident Daughter*).

NOTES

Part 1

CJ's misconduct would become public: Brent Detwiler Documents, https://tinyurl.com/5eaawsx7, BrentDetwiler.com.

In the months that followed: See Mark Galli, "We Need an Independent Investigation of Sovereign Grace Ministries," *Christianity Today*, March 22, 2018, https://tinyurl.com/yy4aph7d; Bob Allen, "Sovereign Grace Churches Says No to Outside Investigation of Abuse," Baptist News Global, April 17, 2019, https://tinyurl.com/mv6phfxt.

Part 2

The original sin of being born female: Quoted in Christiane Northrup, *Women's Bodies, Women's Wisdom* (New York: Bantam, 1998), 4.

Part 5

For centuries, men have projected their inner image of femininity: Marion Woodman, with Kate Danson, Mary Hamilton, and Rita Greer Allen, *Leaving My Father's House: A Journey to Conscious Femininity* (Boston: Shambhala, 1992), 1.

So long as a woman accepts a man's archetypal projection: Woodman et al., *Leaving My Father's House*, 26.

Living by principles: Marion Woodman, *Addiction to Perfection* (Toronto: Inner City Books, 1982), 61.

Part 6

Each of us must recognize where we have cooperated with our own oppression: Northrup, *Women's Bodies, Women's Wisdom*, 25.

Most modern civilizations are characterized by the belief that intellect is superior to emotions: Northrup, *Women's Bodies, Women's Wisdom*, 4.

To improve our lives: Northrup, *Women's Bodies, Women's Wisdom*, 20.

When we acknowledge our needs: Northrup, *Women's Bodies, Women's Wisdom*, 20.

In finding our own story: Woodman et al., *Leaving My Father's House*, 6.

The body recognizes the conscious truth: Woodman et al., *Leaving My Father's House*, 17.

Part 7

Love is the root of everything: *Won't You Be My Neighbor*, directed by Gordon Neville (Focus Features, 2018).

Perfection belongs to the gods: Woodman, *Addiction to Perfection*, 51.

Personal Bill of Rights: Edmund J. Bourne, *Anxiety and Phobia Workbook* (Oakland, CA: New Harbinger Publications, 1990).